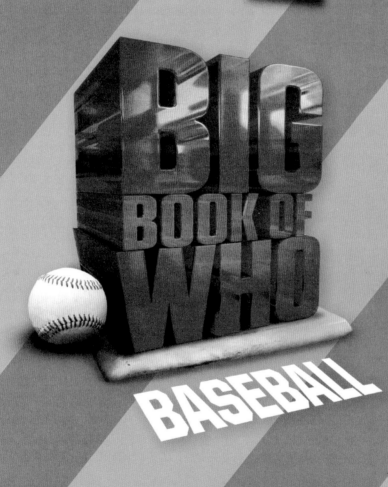

Sports Illustrated KIDS

BIG BOOK OF WHO

BASEBALL

Sports Illustrated KIDS

Writer Mark Bechtel
Designer Drew Dzwonkowski
Photo Editor Linda Bonenfant
Reporter Jeremy Fuchs
Copy Editor Pam Roberts
Production Manager Hillary Leary

Copyright © 2017 Time Inc. Books

Published by Liberty Street, an imprint of
Time Inc. Books
225 Liberty Street
New York, NY 10281

ISBN: 978-1-68330-001-4
Library of Congress Control Number:
2016958270

First edition, 2017

2 QGV 18

10 9 8 7 6 5 4 3 2

We welcome your comments and suggestions
about Time Inc. Books.
Please write to us at:
Time Inc. Books
Attention: Book Editors
P.O. Box 62310
Tampa, FL 33662-2310

timeincbooks.com

Time Inc. Books products may be
purchased for business or
promotional use. For information on
bulk purchases, please
contact Christi Crowley in the
Special Sales Department at
(845) 895-9858.

Batter up!

▶ Baseball is an exciting game played by sluggers who hit mammoth home runs, speedsters who steal bases, and pitchers who throw blazing fastballs. These stars have made baseball our national pastime— and this book tells you all about them. Who was the last Triple Crown winner? Which pitcher has won the most Cy Young Awards? Find out the answers to those questions and many more in this book of the best players from baseball's past and present.

CONTENTS

91

15

32

118

72

3

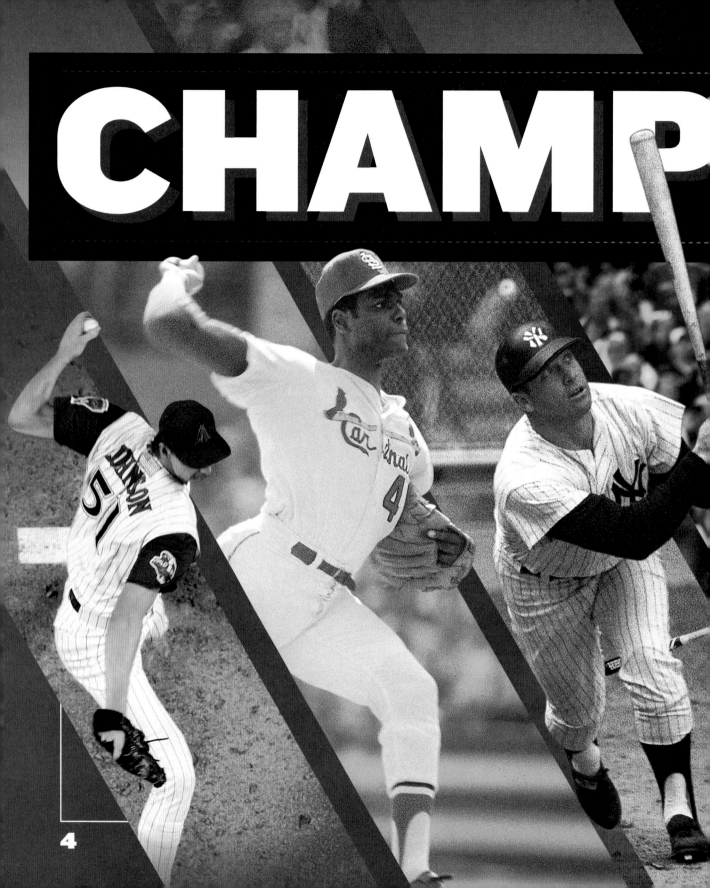

CHAMP

IONS

These clutch performers have starred in the postseason—often more than once.

Who had 14 total bases in one World Series game?

Four players have hit three home runs in a World Series game. But only one of them added two more hits: **Albert Pujols.**

The St. Louis Cardinals' slugger was held hitless by the Texas Rangers in the first two games of the 2011 Fall Classic. When he finally found his stroke in Game 3, he more than made up for his slow start. In addition to his three homers, he added a pair of singles, becoming just the second player to collect five hits in one World Series game. St. Louis won 16–7 to take a 2–1 lead in the series. The Cardinals went on to win the world championship in seven games.

It turned out to be Pujols's last hurrah for St. Louis. In the off-season, the nine-time All-Star signed with the Los Angeles Angels as a free agent.

DID YOU KNOW?

The man who guided the Cardinals to the 2011 title, Tony La Russa, is one of just two managers to win a World Series in both the American and National League. (The other is Sparky Anderson.) La Russa guided the Oakland A's to a championship in 1989. La Russa was known as one of the brightest minds the game has seen. He graduated from law school in 1978. The next year, he got his first job as a major league manager when he was hired by the Chicago White Sox. La Russa's teams won 12 division titles in 33 years. He retired after the 2011 World Series and was inducted into the Hall of Fame three years later.

Super Stat:

12

Consecutive 30-homer seasons by Pujols to begin his career. That's the longest streak ever.

Super Stat:

40

Career World Series RBIs for Mantle, the most ever. He also holds the mark with 123 total bases.

Who hit the most home runs in World Series history?

During his career, **Mickey Mantle** was known for hitting big home runs. *Big* meaning that they traveled far (one went 565 feet). But also *big* meaning that they came in important situations. No situation is more important than a World Series game. And that is when the centerfielder was at his best. Mantle hit 18 Fall Classic home runs, more than any other slugger.

Of course, it helped that he played in so many pivotal games. During his 18-season career, the Mick powered the New York Yankees to the World Series 12 times—and won seven championships.

Which hometown hero was named MVP of the LCS and World Series in the same year?

A handful of players have taken home trophies as most valuable player of both the League Championship series and World Series, but only **David Freese** has done it for his hometown team. The native of the St. Louis suburbs had a monster postseason for the Cardinals in 2011. In the League Championship Series, he hit three homers and had a .545 batting average against the Milwaukee Brewers. In the World Series, he hit a game-tying two-run double in the bottom of the ninth inning of Game 6 with the Cards facing elimination. He then won the game with a walk-off home run in the 11th inning. St. Louis won the Series the next night behind Freese's two RBIs.

Freese also starred in the Cardinals' first-round series. He had a four-RBI outing in Game 4. But there is no MVP award in Division Series play, so he had to be content with two trophies (and one ring).

Super Stat:

21

Runs batted in by Freese in the 2011 playoffs, the most in MLB history in a single postseason.

Who was the ace of the unlikeliest world champs?

The 1969 World Series was won by a team that is known today as the Miracle Mets. Entering the season, New York had never finished higher than ninth in the 10-team National League. But behind pitcher **Tom Seaver,** who won 25 games in the regular season, the Mets won 100 games. They made it all the way to the World Series, where they toppled the Baltimore Orioles in five games. Seaver threw a complete game in New York's 2–1, 10-inning win in Game 4. For his performance, Tom Terrific was named Sportsman of the Year by SPORTS ILLUSTRATED.

FAST FACT: The only other postseason no-hitter was thrown by Roy Halladay of the Phillies in a 2010 Division Series game.

Who is the only pitcher to throw a perfect game in the World Series?

In 1954, Baltimore Orioles pitcher **Don Larsen** had an awful 3–21 record. Two years later, after being traded to the New York Yankees, he threw the greatest game in baseball history. Facing the Brooklyn Dodgers in Game 5 of the 1956 World Series, Larsen retired every hitter he faced. The righty needed just 97 pitches, and went to a three-ball count on only one hitter. (In his other start in that series, he walked four hitters in less than two innings.)

After Larsen struck out pinch hitter Dale Mitchell to end the perfect game, his catcher, Yogi Berra, famously jumped into his arms. The Yankees went on to win the series in seven games. Larsen helped New York to another title in 1958, when he had a 0.96 ERA in two games against the Milwaukee Braves.

Who was the MVP when the Kansas City Royals ended their 30-year championship drought?

In the 2014 World Series, **Salvador Perez** of the Kansas City Royals made the final out of the decisive seventh game with the tying run on third base. The following October, he made up for his failure to come through in the clutch. In the 2015 Fall Classic against the New York Mets, the Royals catcher drove in the tying run in the bottom of the ninth inning of Game 5. He then started the game-winning rally with a single two innings later, as the Royals sewed up their first title since 1985. Perez joined Pablo Sandoval of the 2014 San Francisco Giants as the only World Series MVPs to hail from Venezuela.

FAST FACT:
The 2015 World Series was the first to feature two teams that were formed during baseball's expansion era, which started in 1961.

Who was the last pitcher to win three games in a single World Series?

In 2001, the man called the Big Unit just got better as the year rolled on. In the regular season, Randy Johnson of the Arizona Diamondbacks won 21 games, led the National League in ERA, and struck out 372 batters. (Only two pitchers have rung up more strikeouts in a season since 1900.) In the first round of the playoffs, the 6'10" lefthander stepped up his game. He went 2–0 with a 1.13 ERA against the Atlanta Braves. Somehow he topped that performance in the World Series.

Against the heavily favored New York Yankees, Johnson appeared in three games—and was the winning pitcher in all of them. The future Hall of Famer gave up just two runs in 17⅓ innings, while striking out 19 hitters. His ERA was a sterling 1.04.

DID YOU KNOW?

Thanks to the heroics of Randy Johnson, the Arizona Diamondbacks won the World Series in just their fourth season. Here are the franchises that won a championship the fastest (since 1961, when the majors expanded).

Arizona Diamondbacks
4 years

Florida Marlins
5 years

New York Mets
8 years

Super Stat:

10.61

Strikeouts per nine innings for Randy Johnson during his career, the best rate in major league history.

Who had the most strikeouts in one World Series game?

The 1968 season was known as the Year of the Pitcher. And no one was more responsible for that than **Bob Gibson.** The St. Louis Cardinals's ace had the lowest ERA in modern history (1.12), and he threw 13 shutouts.

Facing baseball's best band of sluggers, the Detroit Tigers, in Game 1 of the '68 World Series, Gibson whiffed a record 17 hitters in a 4–0 win. He followed that up with 10 more K's in Game 4. But he was outdueled in the decisive seventh game, keeping him from winning a third World Series ring.

Thanks largely to Gibson's dominance, the pitcher's mound was lowered by five inches in 1969 to give hitters more of an advantage.

FAST FACT: Before joining the Cardinals, Gibson played one season for basketball's Harlem Globetrotters.

Who has appeared in the most playoff games?

As a 22-year-old rookie in 1996, **Derek Jeter** made his first postseason appearance with the New York Yankees. It became a regular occurrence. By the time Jeter's career ended in 2014, the shortstop had played in 158 playoff games—almost an entire season's worth!

In his 19 full seasons in the big leagues, Jeter failed to make the postseason only three times. The surefire Hall of Famer had a .308 average and hit 20 home runs on the sport's biggest stage. He also made several memorable defensive plays.

Jeter was named the Most Valuable Player of the 2000 World Series in which the Yankees beat the New York Mets. That gave Jeter his fourth career ring. He'd go on to win his fifth and final title with the Yankees in 2009.

Super Stat:

12

Consecutive postseason appearances for the Yankees (1996–2007), the longest run in history.

15

Who pitched with a bloody ankle to keep the Red Sox alive in the 2004 postseason?

The Boston Red Sox entered the 2004 season looking to win the franchise's first world championship in 86 years. Once the American League Championship Series got underway, it looked like that streak was going to reach 87 years. Boston lost the first three games to the New York Yankees. But the Red Sox stormed back to win the next two, setting up a pivotal Game 6.

There was one problem: The scheduled pitcher, **Curt Schilling,** was suffering from a serious ankle injury. Doctors performed a procedure on Schilling's ankle before the game, but the stitches didn't hold. After a few innings, Schilling's sock was partially soaked with blood. Despite the injury, which forced Schilling to limp when he had to field the ball, he lasted seven innings. He allowed just one run, and Boston won 4–2. The next night, the Red Sox won Game 7 to complete their comeback. They then faced the St. Louis Cardinals in the World Series. Schilling pitched another gem in Game 2, and the Sox swept the Redbirds to break their eight-decade curse.

Super Stat:

$92,613

Amount of the winning bid for Schilling's bloody sock when he auctioned it off in 2013.

FAST FACT:
The 2004 Red Sox are the only team in history to win a postseason series after losing the first three games.

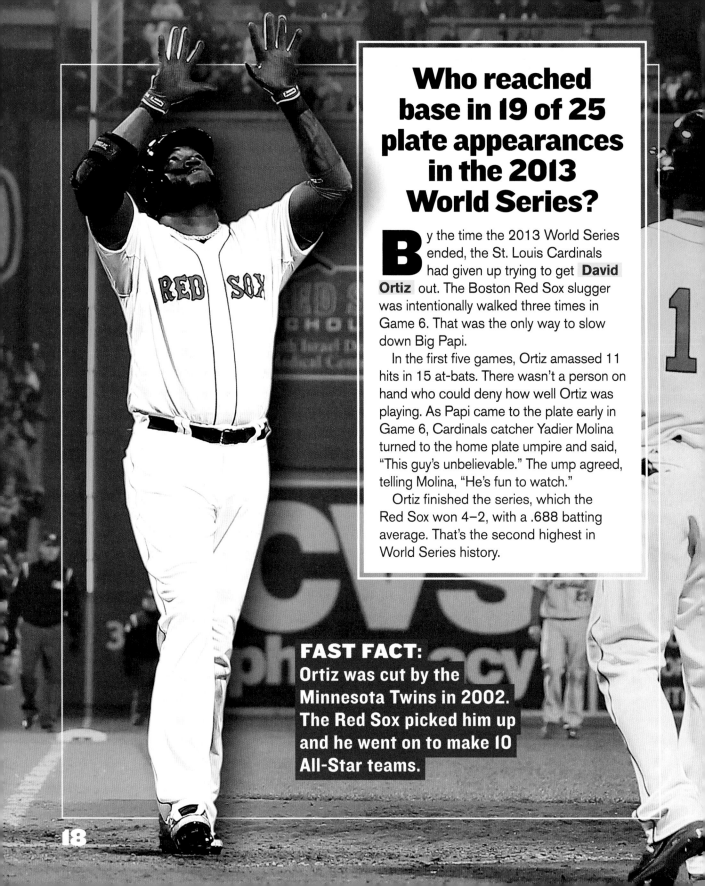

Who reached base in 19 of 25 plate appearances in the 2013 World Series?

By the time the 2013 World Series ended, the St. Louis Cardinals had given up trying to get **David Ortiz** out. The Boston Red Sox slugger was intentionally walked three times in Game 6. That was the only way to slow down Big Papi.

In the first five games, Ortiz amassed 11 hits in 15 at-bats. There wasn't a person on hand who could deny how well Ortiz was playing. As Papi came to the plate early in Game 6, Cardinals catcher Yadier Molina turned to the home plate umpire and said, "This guy's unbelievable." The ump agreed, telling Molina, "He's fun to watch."

Ortiz finished the series, which the Red Sox won 4–2, with a .688 batting average. That's the second highest in World Series history.

FAST FACT:
Ortiz was cut by the Minnesota Twins in 2002. The Red Sox picked him up and he went on to make 10 All-Star teams.

FAST FACT:
After graduating from high school at 16, Rivera worked six days a week on his father's fishing boat.

Super Stat:

652

ular season saves for Rivera his 19 seasons with the Yankees, the most in baseball history.

Which reliever has saved the most playoff games?

For nearly two decades, opponents of the Yankees knew that the key to beating the Bronx Bombers was getting an early lead. Because they could forget about staging a late comeback—especially with **Mariano Rivera** on the mound.

A great closer thrives in tight situations, so it's not a surprise that Rivera—the best stopper in baseball history—was even better in the playoffs than in the regular season. He saved 42 games in the postseason. That's 24 more than any other pitcher. And Rivera did it in a dominating fashion. His ERA in the playoffs was 0.70, and in 141 innings he gave up just two home runs.

Who threw the longest shutout in a World Series–clinching game?

When the world championship is on the line, players aren't afraid of working overtime. Jack Morris proved that in 1991. The Minnesota Twins starter—who had already made two starts totaling 13 innings—took the hill in the decisive seventh game against John Smoltz of the Atlanta Braves. The pitchers took turns shutting down opposing hitters.

Smoltz, who went on to a Hall of Fame career, left in the eighth inning with the score 0–0, but Morris kept plugging away. He was still on the hill in the tenth inning, when he set the Braves down in order. In the bottom of the inning, pinch hitter Gene Larkin singled with the bases loaded, finally breaking the deadlock and giving the Twins the title. Morris, who made history with his extra-inning shutout, was named MVP of the series.

Super Stat:

4

Postseason wins with the Twins for Morris. It's the most in franchise history — even though he spent only one season with the team.

FAST FACT: For the second time ever, the home team wo every game in the 1991 World Series. The first time was 1987—when the Twins also won.

20

Who was on the mound when the Brooklyn Dodgers finally beat the New York Yankees?

Seven times between 1941 and 1956, the Brooklyn Dodgers faced their local rivals in the World Series. They lost six. It might have been all seven had it not been for **Johnny Podres.**

In the 1955 Fall Classic, the teams split the first three games, setting up a winner-take-all showdown at Yankee Stadium. Podres got the call to start for the Dodgers. He had won only nine games in the regular season, but he had beaten the Yankees in Game 3, which Brooklyn won handily. The Yankees had been world champs in five of the previous six seasons, but the 23-year-old Podres shut them down again. Podres scattered eight hits and allowed only two runners to reach third base.

Brooklyn finally had its first—and only—title. The Dodgers moved to Los Angeles three years later.

Which pitcher has the most World Series wins?

They were called the Bronx Bombers for a reason. The New York Yankees of the 1950s and 1960s could smash the ball. But you can't win without pitching, and that's where **Whitey Ford** came in. As a 21-year-old rookie he won the deciding game of the 1950 World Series. He soon became a postseason fixture, starting 22 Fall Classic games—and winning 10 of them. Ford, who was a part of six world championship teams, might have picked up a few more wins, but he missed the 1951 and '52 seasons because he was serving in the Army during the Korean War.

Who is the youngest pitcher to throw a World Series shutout?

For years the Baltimore Orioles were known for their starting pitching—thanks largely to **Jim Palmer.** The righthander broke into the O's rotation in 1966. He promptly won 15 games and earned a start in Game 2 of the World Series against the Los Angeles Dodgers. Nine days before his 22nd birthday he outdueled Hall of Famer Sandy Koufax; Palmer went the distance in a 6–0 win. His fellow Baltimore pitchers must have taken notice. Wally Bunker and Dave McNally followed suit with shutouts of their own, as the Orioles won in a sweep. Los Angeles, which had won 95 games in the regular season, didn't score a run over the final 33⅓ innings of the series.

FAST FACT:
Palmer is the only pitcher to win a **World Series game in three separate decades.**

Super Stat:

0

Grand slams allowed by Palmer in his major league career, which spanned 19 years and 558 games.

Who set the record for stolen bases in a World Series twice?

St. Louis Cardinals speedster **Lou Brock** put on a record-setting performance in the 1967 World Series, stealing seven bases in seven games. No one could call it a fluke, because the following season he did the same thing. Of course, Brock couldn't dazzle with his speed on the basepaths unless he got on base. In 1967, he had a .414 batting average. He was even better the next year, hitting .464.

Brock's heady baserunning helped him lead each series in runs scored. He never appeared in another World Series, but when he retired in 1979 he was a member of the 3,000-hit club and he had a record 938 steals. That mark has since been broken (by Rickey Henderson), but no one has matched his Series steals.

Super Stat:

8

National League stolen base crowns won by Brock, all of which came in a nine-year span (1966–1974).

Who homered on three consecutive pitches in the 1977 World Series?

Before the 1977 season, the New York Yankees signed free agent **Reggie Jackson** to what was then a huge contract: $2.96 million over five years. It took him three swings to prove he was worth the money.

The Yankees led the Los Angeles Dodgers three games to two heading into Game 6 of the World Series. The Dodgers led 3–2 in the fourth inning when Jackson hit a three-run homer on the first pitch of his at-bat against Burt Hooton to put New York in front. The next inning, he hit the first pitch he saw from reliever Elias Sosa out of the park for a two-run homer. In the eighth, Jackson removed any doubt about who would win the game with a 475-foot home run on the first pitch thrown to him by Charlie Hough. The Yankees sewed up the series with the 8–4 win, giving them their first world championship in 15 years.

Super Stat:

2,597

Career strikeouts for Jackson. One of the best sluggers in the game, Jackson liked to swing hard. It meant a lot of homers—and strikeouts.

FAST FACT:
Jackson's postseason heroics earned him the nickname Mr. October.

DID YOU KNOW?

Jackson's power display in 1977 helped give the Yankees their 21st World Series win. He helped them win again in 1978. Since then, New York has taken five more World Series trophies, giving them the most ever. Here are the all-time leading franchises.

New York Yankees
27

St. Louis Cardinals
9

Philadelphia/ Oakland Athletics
8

FAST FACT:
Bumgarner is one of two pitchers to win three World Series titles by the age of 25.

Who has the lowest career ERA in World Series history?

R est? Who needs rest? Certainly not **Madison Bumgarner.** In the 2014 World Series, the San Francisco Giants lefthander followed up a win in Game 1 over the Kansas City Royals with a complete game shutout in Game 5. For most pitchers, that would mean the end of the season. But two days later, Bumgarner came out of the bullpen to throw five scoreless innings of relief as the Giants eked out a win in the deciding seventh game.

Those shutout five innings brought Bumgarner's 2014 playoff total to 52⅔, the most in a single postseason. And they lowered Bumgarner's career World Series ERA to a tiny 0.25. In 36 innings, he gave up one run: a solo homer to Kansas City's Salvador Perez in 2014.

DID YOU KNOW?

Bumgarner doesn't just baffle hitters; he often shows them how it's done. He's such a good hitter that he tried to get a spot in the 2016 Home Run Derby. He's hit 14 home runs in his career, including a pair of grand slams.

Who hit the most dramatic World Series home run?

When **Joe Carter** came to the plate in the ninth inning of Game 6 of the 1993 World Series, his Toronto Blue Jays were trailing the Philadelphia Philles 6–5. But the Jays had two men on base, meaning that Carter had a chance to win the game—and the series—with one swing of the bat.

With the count two balls and one strike, Phillies pitcher Mitch Williams threw a wicked slider that Carter swung at and missed badly. On the next pitch, he decided to sneak a fastball past Carter. But the All-Star rightfielder wasn't fooled. He belted it down the leftfield line, where it cleared the fence. The three-run homer gave Toronto an 8–6 win and a four-games-to-two victory in the series. It marked the first time that a World Series ended on a come-from-behind walk-off home run.

Years later, Carter said that when he was a little kid, he wrote down his ultimate fantasy: "My dream is to hit a home run to win the World Series." So there's more proof that dreams do come true!

Super Stat:

1

Teams from outside of the United States that have won a World Series: the Blue Jays. The Montreal Expos, who played from 1969–2004, never won a championship.

When they stepped to the plate, these hitters struck fear in the hearts of opposing pitchers.

SUPER
SLUGGI

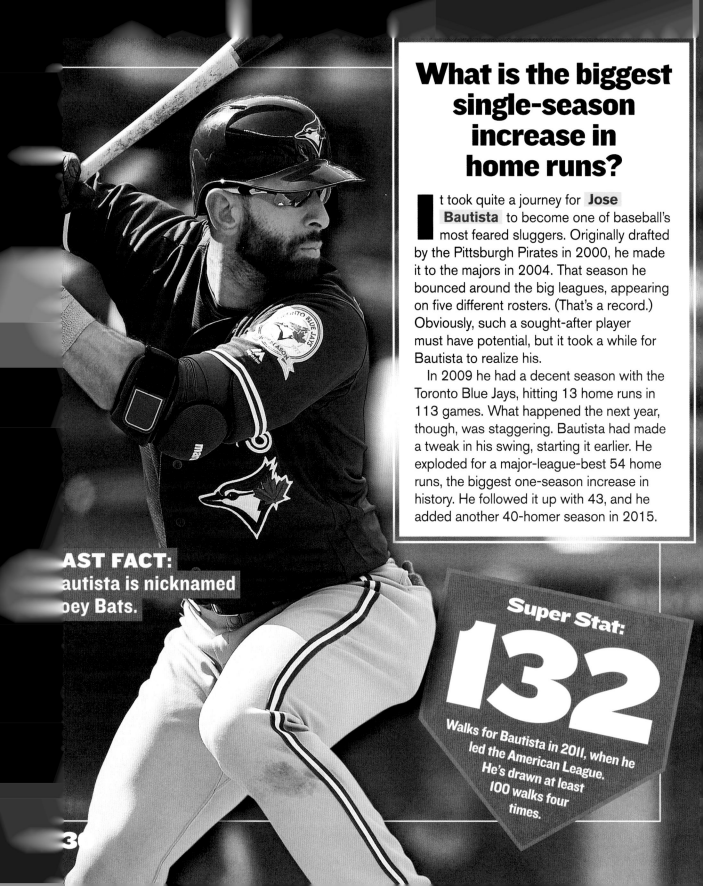

What is the biggest single-season increase in home runs?

It took quite a journey for **Jose Bautista** to become one of baseball's most feared sluggers. Originally drafted by the Pittsburgh Pirates in 2000, he made it to the majors in 2004. That season he bounced around the big leagues, appearing on five different rosters. (That's a record.) Obviously, such a sought-after player must have potential, but it took a while for Bautista to realize his.

In 2009 he had a decent season with the Toronto Blue Jays, hitting 13 home runs in 113 games. What happened the next year, though, was staggering. Bautista had made a tweak in his swing, starting it earlier. He exploded for a major-league-best 54 home runs, the biggest one-season increase in history. He followed it up with 43, and he added another 40-homer season in 2015.

...AST FACT:
...autista is nicknamed
...oey Bats.

Super Stat:

132

Walks for Bautista in 2011, when he led the American League. He's drawn at least 100 walks four times.

Who was the last batter to win his league's Triple Crown?

The three most significant offensive statistics in baseball have long been considered to be batting average, home runs, and runs batted in. It's pretty rare for a player to lead his league in all three in the same season. When he does, it's called a Triple Crown. And the last hitter to wear one was **Miguel Cabrera** of the Detroit Tigers.

Cabrera had already led the league in each category separately. He was the AL home run champ in 2008. He led the league in RBIs in '09, and he had the best batting average in '10. The next year, though, he put it all together, topping the AL with 44 homers, 139 RBIs, and a .330 batting average.

That amazing season made him the American League's first Triple Crown winner since Carl Yastrzemski of the Boston Red Sox in 1967. The last National Leaguer to win one was Joe Medwick of the St. Louis Cardinals, way back in 1937.

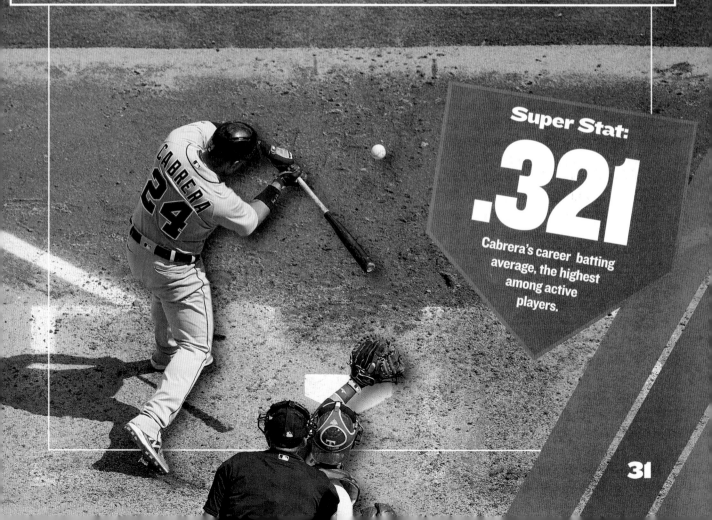

Super Stat:

.321

Cabrera's career batting average, the highest among active players.

Who drove in the most runs in his career?

Because his family was too poor to buy baseball equipment when he was a child, **Hank Aaron** practiced by hitting bottle caps with a broomstick. That helped him develop strong wrists and great eyesight. After hitting something as a small as a bottlecap with something as thin as a broomstick, bashing a ball with a bat was easy. Or at least that's how Aaron made it look.

He broke in with the Milwaukee Braves in 1954 when he was just 20. By his third season, he had won his first batting title. He topped the National League in homers and runs batted in the next year. Aaron went on to become one of the most consistently dangerous hitters in history. From 1955-1971, he drove in at least 90 runs in 15 seasons. (And in the two he missed, he had 86 and 89.) When he finally retired after the 1976 season, he had driven in 2,297 runs.

FAST FACT:
Aaron was known as Hammerin' Hank.

Babe Ruth became baseball's all-time home run king in 1921. When he retired 14 years later, his total stood at 714. The mark wasn't seriously challenged until Aaron came along. As he closed in on Ruth's record, he began receiving threats and hate mail from people who didn't want to see a black player break the record. But Aaron persevered, and on April 8, 1974, he hit his 715th home run. He finished his career with 755. Though his record has been passed by Barry Bonds, Aaron endures as one of baseball's most feared—and respected—sluggers.

Super Stat:

15

Seasons of at least 30 home runs for Aaron, which is tied for the most in history.

Who holds the record for the most RBIs by a switch-hitter?

In his 21-year major league career, **Eddie Murray** was one of the most reliable hitters in the game. Look at his stat lines and you won't see many peaks or valleys. He never led the league in a major offensive category (other than walks) in a full season. But he had 27 home runs and a .283 average as a 21-year-old and 21 homers with a .323 average as a 39-year-old. That's consistency.

Murray was an eight-time All-Star who finished in the top six of the MVP voting for six consecutive years with the Baltimore Orioles. One of the things that made him so dependable was that as a switch-hitter he was dangerous no matter who was on the mound. When he finally hung up his spikes in 1997, he had an average of .293 against righthanded pitchers and .276 against lefties. And his 1,917 RBIs were the most of any switch-hitter in history.

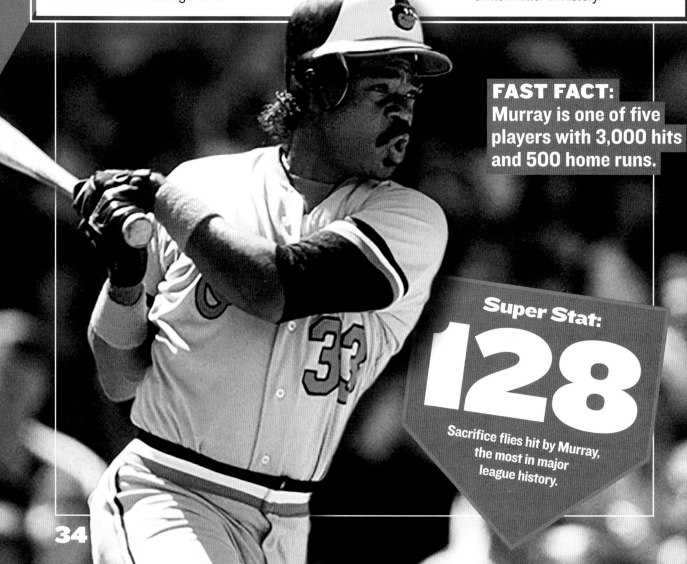

FAST FACT: Murray is one of five players with 3,000 hits and 500 home runs.

Super Stat:
128
Sacrifice flies hit by Murray, the most in major league history.

Who was the first Latin-American player elected to the Hall of Fame?

He was a fantastic hitter and an elite outfielder with a rocket for an arm. But what made **Roberto Clemente** so revered was his character. Clemente was born in Puerto Rico. After moving to the U.S. to play baseball, he remained involved with charities in and around the Caribbean island.

Clemente got his 3,000th career hit in the last week of the 1972 season. Three months later, he died in a plane crash while traveling to Nicaragua to deliver aid to victims of an earthquake. Normally players aren't eligible for the Hall of Fame until five years after their career is over, but an exception was made for Clemente. He was inducted in the summer of 1973.

FAST FACT:
The Roberto Clemente Award is given every year to the player who "best exemplifies the game of baseball, sportsmanship, community involvement and the individual's contribution to his team."

Who was the first player to be named MVP of both leagues?

Before the 1966 season, Cincinnati Reds owner Bill DeWitt traded his star outfielder, **Frank Robinson,** to the Baltimore Orioles. Robinson had been named MVP of the National League in 1961, but DeWitt was afraid that Robinson was past his prime. Bad move.

In his first season with the Orioles, Robinson led the AL with a .316 average, 49 home runs, and 122 RBIs. The Triple Crown winner was named MVP, making him the first player to win the award in both leagues. Robinson went on to play six seasons with Baltimore, and he was able to give the Reds a reminder of just how good he was. The teams met in the 1970 World Series, and Robinson hit a pair of home runs and had four RBIs. Baltimore won the world championship in five games.

Later in his career, Robinson was acquired by the Cleveland Indians, who made him the majors' first black manager while he was still playing. He homered in his first game as manager.

FAST FACT: In Baltimore, Frank played alongside another Hall of Famer with a familiar name: third baseman Brooks Robinson.

Super Stat:

7

Times that Robinson led the league in getting hit by a pitch. He was plunked 198 times in his career. Ouch!

FAST FACT: Bryant is the only player to hit three homers and two doubles in a major league game.

Who out-homered 223 teams during one season in college?

When he was a junior at the University of San Diego in 2013, Kris Bryant bashed 31 home runs. Of the 296 teams in Division I, only 63 hit at least that many. It's no surprise that Bryant received the Golden Spikes Award as the best college player.

But would those numbers translate to professional baseball? In a word, *yes*. After the Chicago Cubs drafted him, Bryant followed up his Golden Spikes Award with the 2014 Baseball America Minor League Player of the Year Award. In 2015 he made it to the majors and was named National League Rookie of the Year.

So what was the next logical step for 2016? That's right, MVP. And Bryant came through, winning the award as he slugged 39 homers and helped the Cubs to their first World Series win in 108 years.

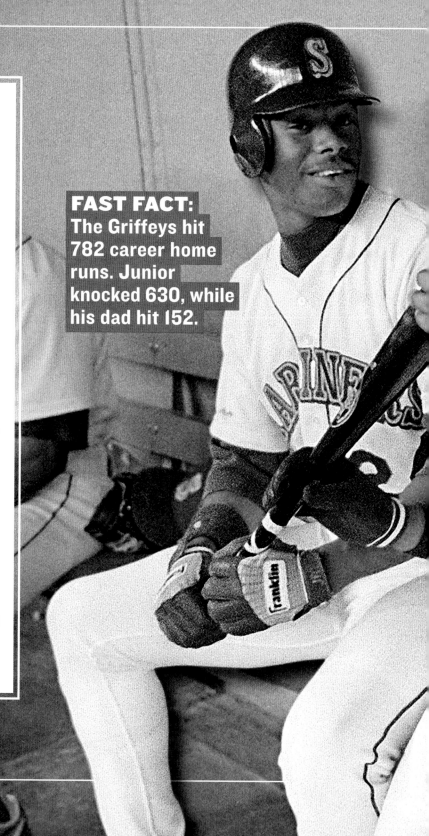

Who is the only player to homer in the same game as his father?

FAST FACT: The Griffeys hit 782 career home runs. Junior knocked 630, while his dad hit 152.

Late in the 1990 season, the Seattle Mariners acquired a 40-year-old veteran with a familiar name: Ken Griffey. His son, 20-year-old **Ken Griffey, Jr.,** was the team's centerfielder. On September 14, the elder Griffey hit a home run in the first inning off of California Angels starter Kirk McCaskill. He was greeted at the plate with a high five by his son, who was the next batter up. Junior promptly followed his dad's lead and hit one over the fence. Like father, like son, indeed.

Years later Junior looked back on the home runs. "I got to play with my dad," he said. "That's the biggest thing that ever happened to me, other than the birth of my children. That's bigger than any record I'll ever set."

- - - - - - - - - - - - - - - - - -

There have been five families in which three generations were represented in the majors. But don't count on the Griffeys joining that list. Ken Griffey Jr. has a son, Trey, who is a stellar athlete. But his sport is football, not baseball. Trey had 11 receptions—including a 95-yard touchdown—for the University of Arizona in 2015. Even though Trey gave up baseball in high school, Seattle drafted him in 2016. But the team did it to honor his father. Trey was taken in round 24, which was junior's number when he was a Mariner.

Super Stat:
99.3
Percentage of Hall of Fame voters who put Griffey Jr. on their ballot the first year he was eligible.

Who holds the AL record for RBIs in a season?

For 14 years, **Lou Gehrig** was a fixture in the New York Yankees lineup. playing in a whopping 2,130 games in a row. The native of New York City joined the Yankees in 1923 and helped them become the Bronx Bombers. The slugger took over as the regular first baseman in 1925. Two years later he had a remarkable season, bashing 47 home runs, driving in 173, and batting .373. (Still, he was somewhat overshadowed by teammate Babe Ruth, who hit 60 home runs.)

In 1931, Gehrig had another monster season. He hit 46 homers and set a league record with 185 RBIs. (He was six short of the major league record, set by Hack Wilson of the Chicago Cubs the year before.) A big reason he knocked in so many runs during his career was that Gehrig was so dangerous with the bases loaded. He had a .370 batting average with the sacks full and banged 23 grand slams. That stood as the big league record for 75 years.

5

Seasons in which Gehrig had at least 400 total bases. He's the only player to do so.

DID YOU KNOW?

Gehrig ended his consecutive-games streak by benching himself on May 2, 1939. He had not been feeling well for some time, and when he didn't get better he went for a series of medical tests. They revealed that Gehrig had a disease called Amyotrophic Lateral Sclerosis (or ALS), which gradually took away his ability to move. Shortly after the disease was diagnosed, Gehrig addressed the crowd at Yankee Stadium. He famously said, "For the past two weeks you have been reading about the bad break I got. Yet today I consider myself the luckiest man on the face of the earth." Gehrig died in 1941. To this day, ALS is commonly known as Lou Gehrig's Disease.

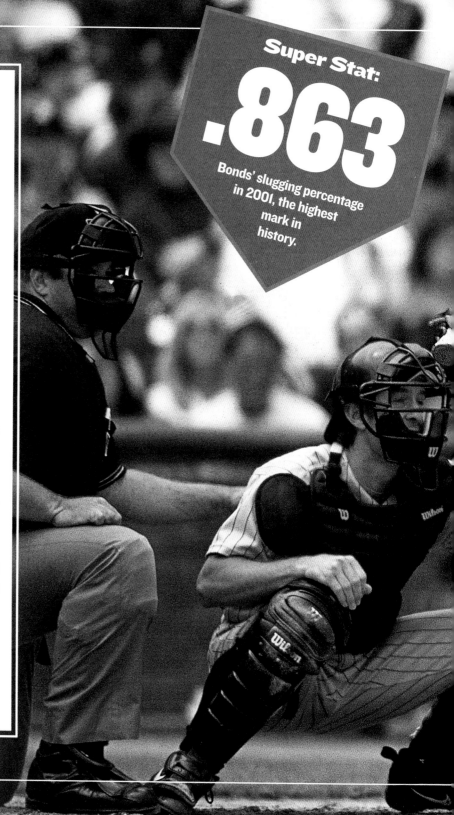

Who is the major leagues' all-time home run king?

O n August 7, 2007, baseball's single-season home run record-holder became its all-time homer king. **Barry Bonds,** who had hit 73 home runs six years earlier, smashed a pitch from Mike Bacsik of the Washington Nationals over the fence at San Francisco's AT&T Park. That gave the Giants slugger 756 homers for his career, one more than Hank Aaron hit. The game was stopped for 10 minutes, and a message from Aaron was played. It congratulated the controversial slugger (who was rumored to have used steroids). Aaron also said he hoped that "the achievement of this record will inspire others to chase their own dreams." The 2007 season was Bonds's last. He finished his career with 762 home runs.

DID YOU KNOW?

What's the best way to keep a slugger from hitting a home run? Don't throw him a pitch he can hit. That was the strategy many pitchers used when facing Bonds. In his career, Bonds walked 2,558 times, easily the most ever. In 2004, he got a free pass 232 times—and 120 of those were intentional walks. In one 1998 game, he was even given an intentional walk when the bases were loaded!

FAST FACT:
Bonds only led the league in home runs twice in his career.

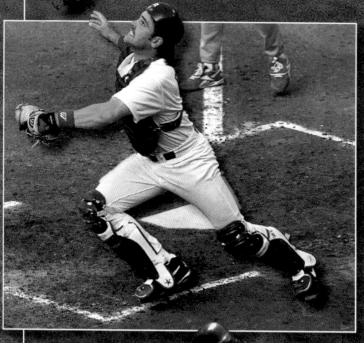

Who holds the record for most homers by a catcher?

In the 62nd round of the 1988 draft, the Los Angeles Dodgers took a first baseman named **Mike Piazza.** They didn't do it because they liked the way he played. They did it as a favor to his father, who was a close friend of Dodgers manager Tom Lasorda. What started out as a nice gesture ended up as a steal of a pick.

Piazza learned to catch and quickly made his way through the Dodgers' system. He arrived in the majors late in the 1992 season and began his career with a walk and a double. The following year he was named the NL Rookie of the Year after hitting .318 with 35 home runs. It was the first of 10 consecutive seasons of at least 24 homers. On May 5, 2004, he hit his 352nd home run as a catcher, breaking the record held by Carlton Fisk.

FAST FACT:
Piazza is one of four players to hit a ball completely out of Dodger Stadium.

Who has the record for most homers by a player who spent his entire career with one team?

Based on his first season with the Philadelphia Phillies, you never would have guessed that **Mike Schmidt** was going to stick around. He hit just .196 and struck out 136 times in 132 games in 1972. But he quickly found his stroke and was a fixture at third base in Philly for more than 15 years. The three-time MVP led the National League in homers eight times, and retired with 548 home runs—all in a Phillies uniform.

FAST FACT: Schmidt is one of 16 players to hit four home runs in one game.

Who won the most consecutive home run titles?

To say that **Ralph Kiner** got his career off to a good start is an understatement. As a rookie with the Pittsburgh Pirates in 1946, he smacked a league-high 23 homers. The next year he hit 51, again leading the league. He kept it up for the next five years, topping the league in home runs seven straight times.

The streak came to an end in 1953, when Kiner was traded to the Chicago Cubs in the middle of the season. He still ended up with 35 home runs, but back injuries were beginning to take a toll on him. After the 1955 season, which he spent with the Cleveland Indians, Kiner retired. He was just 32 years old, and he had hit 369 home runs in his 10-year career. Kiner went on to become a broadcaster for the New York Mets, known for saying things like, "Solo homers usually come with no one on base."

FAST FACT: In 1991, Winfield became the oldest player (40) to hit for the cycle.

Which Hall of Famer was drafted by teams in three sports?

It's always nice to have options. When he left the University of Minnesota **Dave Winfield** had a big decision to make. He had been a basketball star for the Golden Gophers, helping them win the Big Ten championship in 1972. The Atlanta Hawks of the NBA picked him in the fifth round in 1973, and the Utah Stars of the American Basketball Association took him in the fourth. And even though he didn't play football in college, Winfield was drafted by the Minnesota Vikings in the 17th round.

But Winfield elected to sign with the San Diego Padres, who made him the fourth overall selection. It turned out to be a good move. In a 22-year career with six teams, Winfield amassed 3,110 hits and 465 home runs, and he was elected to the Hall of Fame.

Which three-time MVP began his pro career as a pitcher?

When he was a minor league pitcher, Stan Musial would occasionally play in the outfield. But when he banged up his left shoulder trying to make a catch on a fly ball, his career on the mound came to an end.

Pitching's loss turned out to be hitting's gain. Musial went on to enjoy a 22-year career with the St. Louis Cardinals in which he banged out 3,630 hits and 475 home runs. He was also known as one of the great gentlemen the game has ever seen. Asked why he always seemed so happy, he once replied, "If you had a .331 lifetime batting average, you'd be happy all the time too."

Super Stat:

1,815

Career hits by Musial at home. That's the exact same number he had on the road.

Which Negro leagues slugger smacked nearly 800 home runs?

There's an old story that **Josh Gibson** once hit a ball so far that it disappeared into the Pittsburgh sky. The next day during a game between the same two teams in Washington, a ball dropped from the heavens and a fielder caught it. The umpire pointed at Gibson and said, "You're out! In Pittsburgh, yesterday."
Of course the story isn't true, but it shows the respect Gibson had as a power hitter. Unable to play in the majors because he was black, Gibson played in the Negro leagues and in Latin America. Full stats don't exist, but it's estimated that Gibson hit 800 homers—more than any big leaguer.

FAST FACT:
Gibson is credited with hitting a home run in Yankee Stadium that traveled 580 feet.

Who is the only catcher to win three batting titles?

They are often valued more for their defense, but catchers can swing the bat, too. And few have swung it as well as **Joe Mauer.** Between 2006 and 2009, he led the American League in batting average three times. His best season was 2009, when he batted .365 with 28 homers and 96 RBIs. He was named the league's MVP— and he also won his second Gold Glove.

Mauer did it all for the Minnesota Twins, his hometown team. He grew up in St. Paul, not far from where the team plays. The Twins made him the first overall pick in 2001, and he broke into the lineup three years later.

FAST FACT:
Mauer signed a letter of intent to play quarterback at Florida State but elected to play baseball when the Twins made him the first overall pick in the 2001 draft.

Which slugger has won a Gold Glove in each of his first four seasons?

I t's been a perfect start in the field for Colorado Rockies third baseman **Nolan Arenado.** Four seasons, four Gold Gloves. (The only other players to start their careers with four straight Gold Gloves are catchers Johnny Bench and Charles Johnson and outfielder Ichiro Suzuki.) Gold isn't the only precious metal that Arenado has acquired. He won Silver Slugger Awards (as the best hitter at his position) in 2015 and 2016. In each of those seasons he led the National League in home runs and RBIs. Not bad for a 25-year-old who was originally a shortstop.

Who was nicknamed "Home Run" despite never hitting more than 12 in a season?

T he first dominant slugger in the majors was **Frank Baker,** who won four straight American League home run crowns for the Philadelphia Athletics from 1911–14. In those four seasons, he combined to hit a total of 42 bombs. If he had hit 42 home runs in 2016, he wouldn't even have led the AL. (Mike Trumbo of the Baltimore Orioles had 47.)

Baker played in a different time, in what is known as the dead-ball era. Homers were rare for many reasons, including the fact that baseballs were used and reused until they were virtually falling apart—and so dirty they were nearly impossible to see. The muscular Baker had a secret weapon: He used a massive 52-ounce bat. Most players today use bats that weigh around 32 ounces.

Who is the most recent member of the 40-40 club?

Sluggers are often expected to be big, muscular guys who are known for power, not speed. But there are exceptions. Four players have hit 40 home runs and swiped 40 bases in the same season: Jose Canseco (1988), Barry Bonds (1996), Alex Rodriguez (1998), and **Alfonso Soriano** (2006).

Soriano spent only one season with the Washington Nationals, but he made it a memorable one. On September 16, 2006, he stole second base, his 40th of the year, to go with his 45 homers. He'd finish the year with 46 home runs, 41 steals—and 41 doubles, making him the only 40-40-40 member in history.

FAST FACT: Soriano began his professional career playing for the Hiroshima Toyo Carp in Japan.

Who hit the most extra-inning home runs?

He was dangerous no matter what the situation was. But **Willie Mays** was especially dangerous when the game was on the line. Of his 660 home runs, 22 came in extra innings. In fact, Mays set a record homering in 16 different frames (every inning from the first through the 16th).

Mays began his career in the Negro leagues as a 16-year-old. He burst onto the scene in the major leagues as a 20-year-old for the New York Giants in 1951. Mays was one of the most complete players in history. In addition to hitting for power, he had a career average of .302. He also led the National League in stolen bases four times. "He could do the five things you have to do to be a superstar: hit, hit with power, run, throw, and field," Hall of Fame manager Leo Durocher said of Mays. "And he had that other magic ingredient that turns a superstar into a super superstar. He lit up the room. He was a joy to be around."

Super Stat:

23

All-Star Game hits for Mays, the most ever. He also scored a record 20 runs.

Mays won 12 consecutive Gold Gloves—and he would have won more had the award been around at the start of his career. They were first handed out in 1957. But by then it was obvious that Mays was the best glove man in centerfield. He proved the point once and for all in the eighth inning of Game 1 of the 1954 World Series. Vic Wertz of the Cleveland Indians sent a huge drive to the deepest part of the Polo Grounds. Mays caught the ball over his shoulder on the dead run. It saved two runs, and the Giants went on to win the game in extra innings. That win propelled them to a sweep of the Series. And the play is now known simply as "The Catch."

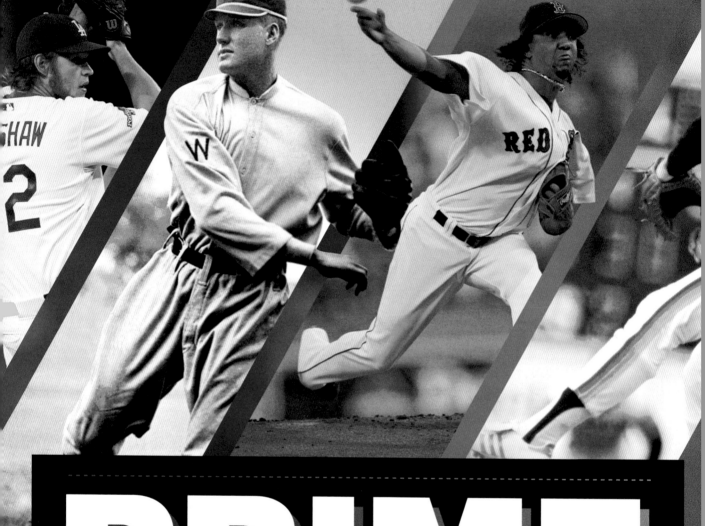

PRIME
PITCHE

It's one of the most important positions in sports. Check out these famous hurlers.

RS

Who was the first pitcher to win two Cy Young Awards?

He didn't have the longest career, but when he was healthy, few pitchers have ever been as dominant as **Sandy Koufax.** The lefthander first appeared for the Brooklyn Dodgers when he was 19. When he was 25—after the team had moved to Los Angeles—he found his stride. He won 18 games, and two years later he won 25, while also posting the best ERA in the National League. Koufax was rewarded by winning his first Cy Young Award.

Two years later, in 1965, Koufax battled through arm pain to win the award again, becoming the first repeat winner. He also threw a perfect game that year and led the Dodgers to a World Series championship. In '66, he won the Cy Young Award for a third time. But shortly after Los Angeles lost the World Series to the Orioles, he announced that he was retiring at age 30 due to arthritis in his pitching elbow.

DID YOU KNOW?

The Cy Young Award is given to the best pitcher in the American and National Leagues. It is named for the pitcher who won a record 511 games in his career. Young died in 1955, and the award was handed out a year later. For the first 11 years the recipient was the best pitcher in the major leagues—meaning that all three times Koufax won the award he was competing against every pitcher in the major leagues. In 1967 the practice of giving the award to the best pitcher in each league began.

Super Stat:
36

Koufax's age when he was inducted into the Hall of Fame. He was the youngest player ever enshrined.

Who once threw a pitch faster than a speeding motorcycle?

Before the invention of the radar gun, it was difficult to tell just how fast a pitcher was throwing the ball. In 1941, **Bob Feller** of the Cleveland Indians was considered the hardest thrower in baseball. In an effort to estimate just how speedy his fastball was, a race was organized. Feller would throw a pitch as a motorcycle passed him. The bike—which was ridden by a police officer— had a 10-foot head start when the ball left Feller's hand, and it was traveling 86 miles per hour. But Feller's heater beat it to the target, which was 60' 6" away. (That's the distance the mound is from home plate.) The pitch was calculated to have traveled 98.6 miles per hour.

When Feller retired in 1956, he had 2,581 strikeouts—and would have had more, but he missed three-and-a-half seasons during his prime to serve in the Navy in World War II.

FAST FACT:
Feller is the only pitcher in history to throw a no-hitter on Opening Day. He did it in 1940.

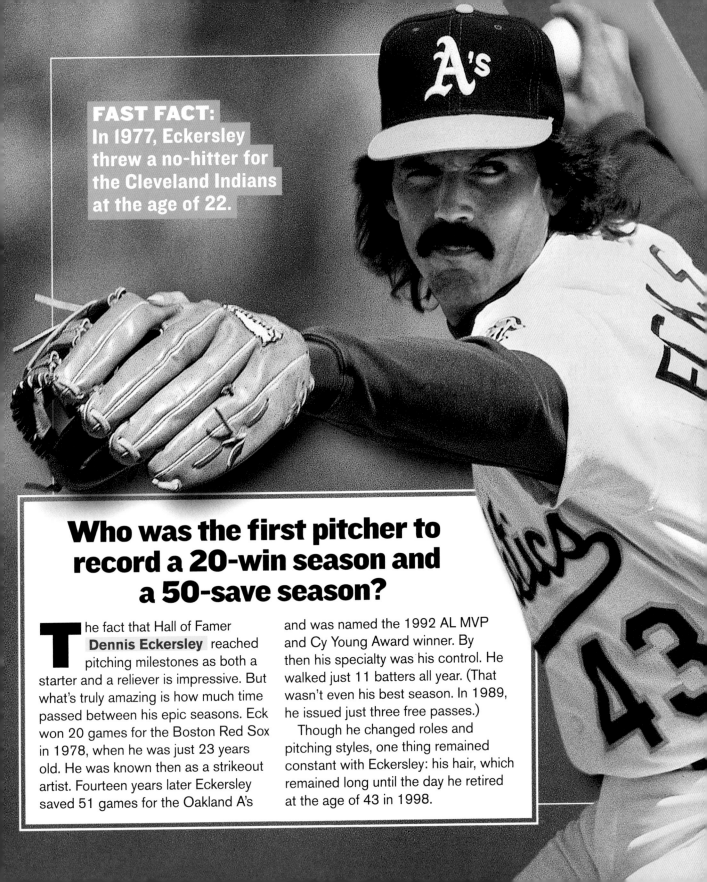

Who was the first pitcher to record a 20-win season and a 50-save season?

The fact that Hall of Famer **Dennis Eckersley** reached pitching milestones as both a starter and a reliever is impressive. But what's truly amazing is how much time passed between his epic seasons. Eck won 20 games for the Boston Red Sox in 1978, when he was just 23 years old. He was known then as a strikeout artist. Fourteen years later Eckersley saved 51 games for the Oakland A's and was named the 1992 AL MVP and Cy Young Award winner. By then his specialty was his control. He walked just 11 batters all year. (That wasn't even his best season. In 1989, he issued just three free passes.)

Though he changed roles and pitching styles, one thing remained constant with Eckersley: his hair, which remained long until the day he retired at the age of 43 in 1998.

Who was the last AL pitcher to be named Most Valuable Player?

Since pitchers have their own award—the Cy Young—it's rare for a hurler to beat out the hitters and be named Most Valuable Player. It has happened, though, including in 2011. That was the year that righthander **Justin Verlander** of the Detroit Tigers won both awards.

Verlander had an amazing season. He won 24 games—the most by an American League pitcher since 1990. He led the league in ERA (2.40) and strikeouts (239) as well. He also gave up the fewest hits per nine innings. The Tigers won 95 games and advanced to the AL Championship Series, where they were beaten by the Texas Rangers. Verlander won the Cy Young Award unanimously. In the MVP race, he beat out Jacoby Ellsbury of the Boston Red Sox, receiving 13 of the 28 first-place votes.

DID YOU KNOW?

Verlander is one of 10 players to win both the MVP and the Cy Young Award in the same season. But he is one of only two to also have been named Rookie of the Year. (Verlander took that award in 2006.) Talk about a packed trophy case!

Which pitcher has won the most Cy Young awards?

Known as Rocket, **Roger Clemens** played for four different teams during his 24-year career. And he was successful with every one of them. In fact, at every stop he's made, Clemens has won a Cy Young Award. He notched his first in 1986 with the Boston Red Sox, and repeated as the winner in 1987 before winning a third in 1991. Six years later he moved on to the Toronto Blue Jays, where he won the trophy in both seasons with the team. Then it was on to the New York Yankees, where he won the award in 2001 thanks to a 20–3 record. Three years later the Texas native moved home, joining the Houston Astros. Despite the fact that he was 41 years old, Clemens put up an 18–4 record and a 2.98 ERA. That was good enough to pick up his seventh Cy Young Award. That's two more than his closest competition, Randy Johnson. (Johnson did do one thing Clemens didn't: He won the award four years in a row.)

Super Stat:
4,672
Career strikeouts for Clemens, the third-most in major league history.

Who was the only pitcher to have 200 wins and 100 saves?

During his 21-year career with the Atlanta Braves, **John Smoltz** was one of the best starting pitchers in the history of the franchise. In 1996, he led the National League with 24 wins. Then he began suffering from arm trouble and became ineffective as a starter. So late in the 2001 season he moved to the bullpen. The following year, his first as a full-time closer, Smoltz set an NL record with 55 saves. Two more great seasons out of the bullpen made it clear that he had regained his stuff, so in 2005 he was moved back into the starting rotation. In 2006 he proceeded to lead the league in wins again, this time at age 39. Smoltz finally retired in 2009, and he was elected to the Hall of Fame in his first year of eligibility.

Who holds the rookie record for saves?

Though he was a rookie in 2011, **Craig Kimbrel** was no stranger to the majors. The year before, the 23-year-old had been called up to the Atlanta Braves four times. He struck out a whopping 40 batters in just 20⅓ innings—but he also walked 16. The following year, the team was in need of a closer. Luckily for the Braves, Kimbrel got his wildness under control. In 77 innings, he struck out 127 hitters and walked just 32. Kimbrel notched 46 saves, the first of four consecutive seasons in which he led the league. And since he had pitched fewer than 30 innings in a season, Kimbrel was still considered a rookie. So he took home Rookie of the Year honors—and etched his name in the record book for most saves by a first-year player.

Super Stat:
318
Games Kimbrel needed to reach 200 saves. He is the fastest pitcher to reach that mark.

Which machinelike pitcher is nicknamed Klubot?

After he finished his pregame warmup before Game 1 of the 2016 World Series, Cleveland Indians pitcher **Corey Kluber** did something that shocked his teammates. He smiled.

Kluber is known for not showing emotion, so when he emerged from the bullpen with a grin on his face, the Indians knew something special was in store. Sure enough, Kluber struck out eight Chicago Cubs batters in the first three innings. Cleveland went on to win 6–0.

His steady demeanor earned Kluber the nickname Klubot (think half-man, half-robot). Nothing seems to faze him—he just goes out and gets the job done no matter what the situation. He may not smile much, but he gives Cleveland fans plenty of reason to: He won the Cy Young Award in 2014 and finished third in 2016.

FAST FACT: Kluber was the winning pitcher in the 2016 All-Star Game.

Who has the lowest single-season WHIP in history?

Major league hitters were thriving in 2000. The sport was in the midst of an offensive explosion the likes of which it had never seen. Teams averaged 1.16 home runs per game and the league-wide slugging percentage was .437. Both of those marks were the highest in history.

Someone forgot to tell **Pedro Martinez** that he was pitching in an era that belonged to the hitters. The Boston Red Sox righthander had one of the most remarkable seasons ever in 2000. In 217 innings he allowed just 128 hits and 32 walks. His WHIP of 0.737 was the lowest in major league history. (WHIP measures the number of walks plus hits a pitcher averages per inning pitched.) And it was no fluke. In the nine seasons from 1997 though 2005, Martinez had a WHIP of less than 1.000 six times.

40

Consecutive innings in which Martinez had a strikeout during the 1999 season, the longest streak in history.

DID YOU KNOW?

Martinez won the Cy Young Award as a member of the Montreal Expos (1997) and Boston Red Sox (1999 and 2000). Only four other pitchers have won the award in both leagues: Gaylord Perry (San Diego Padres and Cleveland Indians), Roger Clemens (Red Sox, Toronto Blue Jays, New York Yankees, and Houston Astros), Roy Halladay (Blue Jays and Philadelphia Phillies), and Randy Johnson (Seattle Mariners and Arizona Diamondbacks).

Which fireballer threw seven no-hitters?

Hitters who had to face **Nolan Ryan** knew they shouldn't expect to get many hits. Hall of Famer Reggie Jackson once said, "You just hoped to mix in a walk so you could have a good night and go 0 for 3." Seven times in his 27-year career Ryan held an opposing team hitless for nine innings. And he came close plenty of other times: He had 12 one-hitters.

Ryan threw his first two no-hitters in 1973 for the California Angels. He notched his seventh no-no 18 years later when he was with the Texas Rangers. In that game, the 44-year-old notched an incredible 16 strikeouts. Ryan had one of the hardest fastballs the game has ever seen. In 1974, he threw the first 100-mph pitch ever officially recorded. It was also one of the wildest fastballs the game has ever seen. In addition to his record 5,714 career strikeouts, Ryan walked 2,795 hitters—nearly 1,000 more than any other hurler.

DID YOU KNOW?

When a pitcher strikes out all three batters in an inning on only nine pitches—the fewest number possible—that's known as an immaculate inning. The feat has been accomplished by 77 hurlers, but only four, including Ryan, have done it more than once. Sandy Koufax of the Dodgers had three immaculate innings, while Lefty Grove (Philadelphia A's), Randy Johnson (Astros and Diamondbacks) and Ryan (Mets and Angels) have had two apiece.

Which youngster began his career with 17 straight wins at home?

Because he was born in Cuba, which is just 90 miles from the coast of Florida, **Jose Fernandez** felt at home in Miami. It showed in his pitching. The righthander started his career by going 17–0 at Marlins Park. Fernandez wasn't bad on the road either. He finished in the top 10 in ERA in both of his full major league seasons before he tragically died at age 24 in a boating accident during the 2016 campaign.

Fernandez went to great lengths to make it to the majors. Cuban-born players were forbidden from playing in other countries, so he had to escape the country on a boat. He was unsuccessful the first three times he tried, and after each attempt he was jailed. Fernandez finally made it in 2007. On that trip, he had to jump into the water to save his mother, who fell overboard in rough waters.

Who has the most wins by a lefthanded pitcher?

During the 1940s and 1950s, Milwaukee Braves fans had a saying: "Spahn and Sain and pray for rain." The hope was that with enough rainouts, their ace, **Warren Spahn,** and his teammate Johnny Sain would be able to pitch every game! You can't blame Braves fans for wanting to see Spahn on the mound as often as possible. He was one of the toughest pitchers to hit, and one of the most durable. Spahn's career lasted 21 seasons, and he won at least 20 games in 13 of them—including one stretch of six in a row.

Spahn relied on his brain as much as his arm. His pitching coach once said, "He makes my job easy. Every pitch he throws has an idea behind it."

Super Stat:

35

Home runs hit by Spahn during his career, the most by a National League pitcher.

Who was the only pitcher to lead the majors in ERA four years in a row?

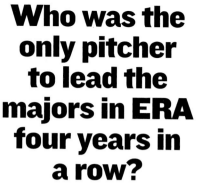

In 2010, **Clayton Kershaw** of the Los Angeles Dodgers had an ERA of 2.91, which ranked ninth in the National League. Not too bad, right? Well, it's actually the *worst* ERA he has put up over a full season in his career. Kershaw led the league every season from 2011 through 2014. It took a spectacular season to end the run. In 2015, his teammate Zack Greinke had a 1.66 ERA, which beat Kershaw's 2.13.

With another great season in 2016, Kershaw lowered his career ERA to 2.37. That's the lowest mark for any starter who has pitched in the last 89 years.

FAST FACT:
Kershaw played center on his high school football team. His quarterback was Matthew Stafford, who now plays for the Detroit Lions.

Which pitcher was responsible for 27 of his team's 59 wins in 1972?

The 1972 Philadelphia Phillies were bad. Very bad. They finished dead last with a .378 winning percentage. And it would have been a lot worse if it weren't for **Steve Carlton.** The imposing lefty won 27 games (meaning the team's other 15 pitchers combined to win 32). He led the league in ERA (1.97) and strikeouts (310).

Carlton had been traded to Philadelphia just before the season. He became a mainstay of the Phillies rotation, and the team gradually improved, notching 101 wins in 1976. In 1980, Carlton led Philadelphia to its first world championship in the team's 97-year existence. He led the Phillies back to the World Series in 1983, the same year he won his 300th game.

Which old-timer won an amazing 59 games in one season?

These days, pitchers take the mound every fifth day or so and hardly ever throw more than 200 innings a season. **Charles Radbourn** would have loved a schedule like that. Back in 1884 his team, the Providence Grays, lost its second best pitcher. So Radbourn volunteered to take the mound for every game. Of the Grays' final 43 games, Radbourn started 40—and he won 36 of them. He finished the season with 678⅔ innings pitched and 59 wins. Legend has it that by the end of the season, his arm was so worn out that he couldn't raise it high enough to comb his hair. It paid off, though, as the Grays made it to the World Series, where they swept the New York Metropolitans. Naturally, Radbourn pitched every inning of the Series and didn't allow an earned run.

Which strikeout artist was known as the Big Train?

For more than 50 years, the 3,000-strikeout club had only one member: **Walter Johnson.** The Washington Senators hurler notched his 3,000th K on July 22, 1923. No one else reached that mark until Bob Gibson in 1974. Known as one of the friendliest men to play the game, Johnson could be ruthless on the mound. He finished his career with 110 shutouts (a major league record) and 417 wins (second to only Cy Young). He led the American League in strikeouts 12 times, including eight years in a row. Following his career, he was voted into the Hall of Fame as part of its first class.

FAST FACT: After he retired, Johnson unsuccessfully ran for the U.S. House of Representatives in 1940.

Who was the last pitcher to strike out 20 hitters in a game?

On May 11, 2016, **Max Scherzer** of the Washington Nationals blew away his old team, the Detroit Tigers. He whiffed 20 hitters in a 3–2 win, becoming the third player to reach that mark in a nine-inning game—and the first since 1998. One Tigers player said facing Scherzer that day was "like a horror film."

As scary as Scherzer was that day, it wasn't even the most dominant performance of his career. In June of 2015, he came within one out of a perfect game against the Pittsburgh Pirates. But with two outs in the ninth inning he hit a batter and had to settle for a no-hitter. Three months later Scherzer threw another no-no. Once again, he didn't walk anyone; the only New York Met to reach did so on an error. And Scherzer had 17 strikeouts that day, the most ever for a pitcher in a no-hitter.

Who threw two no-hitters, including one during the playoffs, in the same season?

I t took **Roy Halladay** 12 seasons to finally make it to the playoffs. So when he got to baseball's biggest stage, he was sure to make the most of it. Against the Cincinnati Reds in the 2010 NL Division Series, Halladay threw a no-hitter. (It was just the second no-hitter in postseason history.) That came four months after he threw a perfect game versus the Florida Marlins. Yes, 2010 was a pretty good year for the big righthander. He finished the season with 21 wins and took home his second career Cy Young Award.

Which flamethrower known as Goose helped pioneer the closer's role?

F or many years, teams would use a variety of pitchers in the late innings of a close game. In the 1970s, though, the strategy of using one pitcher as the "closer" to finish out the game became more popular. One of the most effective relievers of that era was **Goose Gossage.** In the late 1970s, the New York Yankees began using Ron Davis as a "setup man" before turning it over to Gossage to get the final outs. Gossage saved a career-high 33 games in 1979.

Gossage was also one of the first closers to rely on intimidation to get an edge on hitters. He had a scraggly mustache and would stare down hitters before firing hard fastballs. He pitched until he was 43 years old, and in 2005 he became the fifth relief pitcher elected to the Hall of Fame.

Who won at least 15 games for 17 straight seasons?

Few pitchers have been as good as **Greg Maddux.** Even fewer have been as dependable. Maddux won 18 games in 1988 for the Cubs, beginning a 17-season run of picking up at least 15 victories. While he is a member of the 3,000-strikeout club, Maddux wasn't a power pitcher. Rather, he relied on his pinpoint control to keep hitters off balance. How accurate was Maddux? In 1997, he issued just 20 walks—and six of them were intentional.

The brainy Maddux was known as the Mad Professor, and he was always prepared for his opponents. His longtime pitching coach Leo Mazzone once said, "He studies during the four days in between starts, then teaches on the fifth."

Super Stat:

18

Gold Gloves won by Maddux, the most for any player.

These players are known for their antics off the field as well as on it.

COOL CHARAC

CTERS

Which colorful catcher was known as Mr. Baseball?

He certainly wasn't the best player in history, but **Bob Uecker** might be the funniest. He had a batting average of just .200, and he liked to joke about that. "If a guy hits .300 every year, what does he have to look forward to?" he said. "I always tried to stay around .190, with three or four RBIs. And I tried to get them all in September. That way I always had something to talk about during the winter." Uecker had a six-year career that included a World Series win with the St. Louis Cardinals in 1964. "Anybody with ability can play in the big leagues. But to be able to trick people year in and year out the way I did, I think that was a much greater feat," he joked. After his career, he became more famous than he ever had been as a player. He was a frequent guest on talk shows. (Host Johnny Carson jokingly gave him the nickname Mr. Baseball.) He has spent more than 40 years as a commentator for the Milwaukee Brewers.

FAST FACT:
After he retired, Uecker starred for several years in a TV comedy called *Mr. Belvedere.*

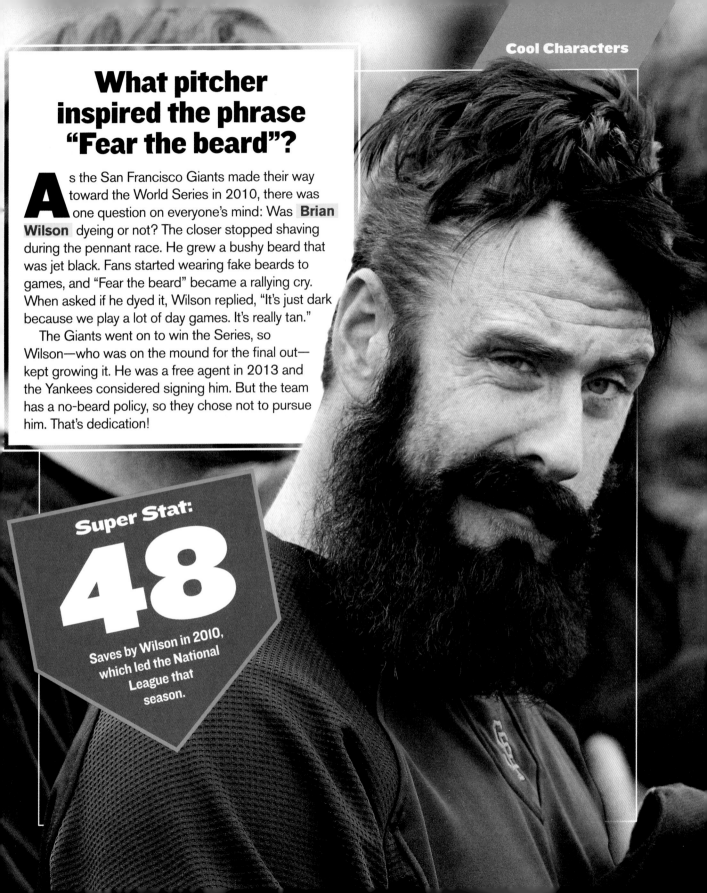

What pitcher inspired the phrase "Fear the beard"?

As the San Francisco Giants made their way toward the World Series in 2010, there was one question on everyone's mind: Was **Brian Wilson** dyeing or not? The closer stopped shaving during the pennant race. He grew a bushy beard that was jet black. Fans started wearing fake beards to games, and "Fear the beard" became a rallying cry. When asked if he dyed it, Wilson replied, "It's just dark because we play a lot of day games. It's really tan."

The Giants went on to win the Series, so Wilson—who was on the mound for the final out—kept growing it. He was a free agent in 2013 and the Yankees considered signing him. But the team has a no-beard policy, so they chose not to pursue him. That's dedication!

Super Stat:

48

Saves by Wilson in 2010, which led the National League that season.

What quotable catcher was thought to be the inspiration for Yogi Bear?

The famous cartoon character Yogi Bear was introduced in 1958. While his creators claim it was a coincidence, one of the most famous players in baseball at that time was a catcher for the New York Yankees with a very similar name: **Yogi Berra.**

The similarities didn't end with their names; they were both stocky guys with memorable ways of speaking. Berra was a zany character, but make no mistake: He was an amazing ballplayer. He played in 18 All-Star Games and was a three-time Most Valuable Player, including 1954 and 1955, when he became the third player to win the award in consecutive seasons.

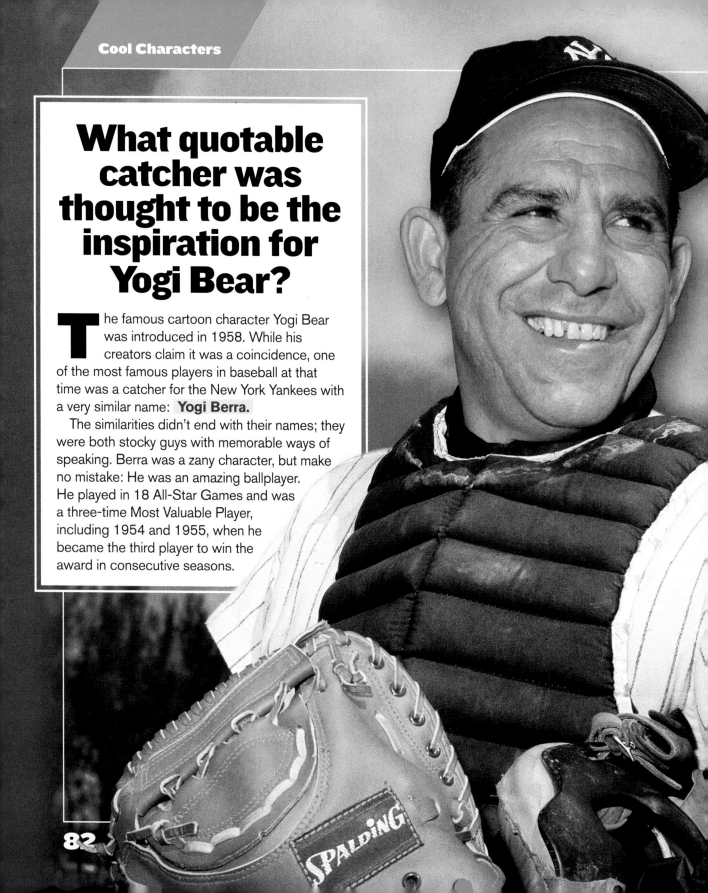

AS YOGI SAID . . .

Berra was one of the most quotable athletes in sports history. Whether he meant it or not, certain Yogi-isms have found their way into the culture canon.

"Ninety percent of this game is half mental."

"I'd give my right arm to be ambidextrous."

"It's tough to make predictions. Especially about the future."

"You give 100 percent in the first half of the game, and if that isn't enough, in the second half you give what's left."

Super Stat:

10

World Series championships won by Berra (all with the Yankees). That's the most of any player.

Which zany pitcher was so far out that he was known as the Spaceman?

In 1971, pitcher **Bill Lee** of the Boston Red Sox was talking to a group of reporters at his locker about one of NASA's missions to the moon. It was a strange topic for a baseball player to be talking about, so when a teammate saw the crowd Lee was drawing—and couldn't get to his locker as a result—he started calling the pitcher Spaceman.

It was a fitting nickname, because sometimes it seemed as if Lee was from another planet. Lee, who pitched lefthanded, didn't see anything strange in his behavior. "You have two hemispheres in your brain—a left and a right side," he explained. "The left side controls the right side of your body and right controls the left half. It's a fact. Therefore, lefthanders are the only people in their right minds."

FAST FACT: Lee played all nine positions in one game for the San Rafael Pacifics, an independent league team, in 2013. Lee was 66 at the time.

Super Stat:

17

Wins for Lee in 1973, when he made the American League All-Star team.

Who appears on the most valuable baseball card ever?

In the early 1900s, tobacco companies began including cards featuring baseball players in their packs of cigarettes. One of the best players of the era was **Honus Wagner.** The Pittsburgh Pirates shortstop would later become a member of the very first Hall of Fame class. He was reportedly also against the idea of having kids buy cigarettes to get

WAGNER, PITTSBURG

his card, so he asked one company to remove his card. (Other reports say he wanted money from the tobacco company.) But a few cards—believed to be somewhere between 50 and 200—had already been produced. Since they were so rare, they have become incredibly valuable. In 2007, a Wagner card that had once been owned by hockey legend Wayne Gretzky was sold for a staggering $2.8 million to the owner of the Arizona Diamondbacks.

Super Stat:

8

Batting titles won by Wagner. No National Leaguer has won more.

85

What pitcher was known for talking to the baseball?

Nicknamed "the Bird" for his resemblance to Sesame Street's Big Bird, **Mark Fidrych** made quite a splash in 1976. The young righthander for the Detroit Tigers nearly threw a no-hitter in his first start, but what really got people's attention were his antics. Fidrych spent a lot of time patting down the dirt on the mound and talking to the baseball. That's right— talking to the baseball! It must have listened. Fidrych went on to win 19 games and lead the American League in ERA. He also was the starting pitcher in the All-Star Game. But knee and arm injuries suffered the next year slowed him down, and he only made 27 more starts before he was released following the 1981 season.

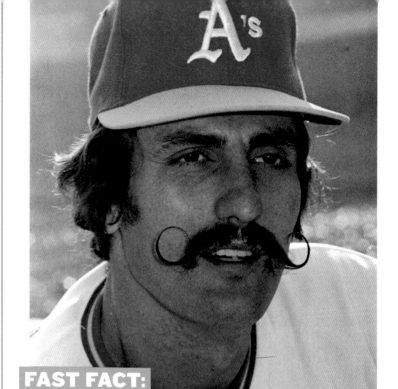

FAST FACT: Fingers had his uniform number retired by two teams: the A's and the Milwaukee Brewers.

Which Hall of Famer led the Oakland A's famed Mustache Gang?

In 1972, Oakland A's slugger Reggie Jackson showed up at spring training with a mustache. So a few teammates followed suit. They thought their manager would make them all shave, but instead the team's owner, Charlie Finley, decided the facial hair would give his team personality. He told the players that anyone who grew a mustache would get a $300 bonus. Reliever **Rollie Fingers** grew a majestic handlebar mustache, which became the most recognizable. The hairy A's played well, and since baseball players are a superstitious bunch, they kept the mustaches. Oakland won the World Series in 1972, 1973, and 1974. And Fingers kept his mustache for the rest of his Hall of Fame career.

What excitable pitcher was known as the Mad Hungarian?

Players do a lot of things to get in their opponents' heads. For relief pitcher **Al Hrabosky,** that meant acting very weird. "I want batters to think I'm crazy," he explained. "I want them to know I'm crazy." His big Fu Manchu mustache helped, but what really made him seem bonkers was his habit of psyching himself up behind the mound. Hrabosky would turn his back to the batter, talk to himself, and then slam the ball into his glove. One time he missed and the ball rolled away, but usually the bizarre tactic paid dividends. Hrabosky—who was nicknamed the Mad Hungarian—was one of the best closers of the 1970s.

Super Stat:

1.66

Hrabosky's ERA in 1975, when he finished third in the Cy Young voting. He won 13 games and had 22 saves.

Who is the only player to appear in a World Series and a Super Bowl?

The first full week of September 1989 was a good one for **Deion Sanders.** The New York Yankees outfielder hit a home run on Tuesday — and scored a touchdown the following Sunday. Sanders was also a football player for the Atlanta Falcons and he returned a punt for a score. The flashy Sanders, who was nicknamed Prime Time, juggled the two sports for nearly a decade. In 1992, he was a member of the Atlanta Braves team that advanced to the World Series. (Sanders hit .533 with five steals in six games.) Two years later he was a cornerback on the San Francisco 49ers team that won Super Bowl XXIX, and he won again the following year with the Dallas Cowboys. Sanders finished his baseball career with a .263 average and 186 stolen bases. He truly shone on the gridiron, though. He was enshrined in the Pro Football Hall of Fame in 2011.

Super Stat:

14

Triples for Sanders in 1992, when he led the National League despite playing in just 97 games.

DID YOU KNOW?

Sanders wasn't the only two-sport star of his era. Before injuries cut his career short, Bo Jackson was an elite slugger for the Kansas City Royals and a bruising running back for the Los Angeles Raiders. He hit a leadoff home run in the 1989 All-Star Game and was voted to the Pro Bowl after the 1990 season (though he couldn't play due to injury). Jackson remains the only player named an All-Star and a Pro Bowler.

FAST FACT:
Sanders attended Florida State, where he was on the baseball, football, and track teams.

Which portly player is known as Kung Fu Panda?

He is shaped like a bear, but that's not the reason that **Pablo Sandoval** is known as Kung Fu Panda. San Francisco Giants teammate Barry Zito gave him the nickname after the animated movie that came out in 2008. "It was about this regular panda that had superpowers," Zito said. "You see Pablo on the street, [and] he kind of looks like a normal guy. Then you get him on the baseball field, and he can do amazing things." Fans responded by wearing panda hats to games.

Sandoval is known for two things: always smiling, and swinging at any pitch. He once jumped up in the air to swing at a knuckleball over his head. Sandoval ended up grounding out, but being a free-swinger has worked out pretty well for him. He has two 20-home run seasons and ended the 2016 season with a .287 career batting average.

Super Stat:

13

Consecutive playoff games in which Sandoval had a hit in 2013 and 2014, a National League record.

8,375

Career assists by Smith, the most ever by a shortstop.

What shortstop began each season with a backflip?

Few players have ever looked like they were having more fun on the field than **Ozzie Smith.** The shortstop, who spent most of his career with the St. Louis Cardinals, celebrated the beginning of each season by running onto the field and doing a backflip. (He also did one on the last day of the season.)

Over the course of his career, Smith gave fans plenty of reason to jump for joy. A speedster who stole at least 25 bases in 14 different seasons, Smith was known as one of the best fielders ever at his position. "I was always hoping they would hit the ball his way because I knew then that my trouble was over," one of his pitchers said. Known as the Wizard of Oz, Smith won the Gold Glove every year from 1980 through 1992. He also swung the bat pretty well. He ended his career with 2,460 hits.

FAST FACT: Smith hit a game-winning home run in the 1985 NL Championship Series—and then didn't homer again for more than two years.

Who was the leader of the St. Louis Cardinals' wacky Gashouse Gang?

The 1934 St. Louis Cardinals were one of the zaniest—and best— teams in history. They were known as the Gashouse Gang, because the rowdy players always seemed to have dirty uniforms, like the greasy clothes of a car mechanic. Their leader was pitcher

Dizzy Dean. Born Jay Hanna Dean, he picked up his nickname in the Army before he began his baseball career. He joined the Cardinals for good in 1932 and proceeded to win 18 games and lead the league in strikeouts. He was the strikeout king in each of the next three seasons as well. Dean was named the National League MVP in 1934, when the Gashouse Gang won 95 games and beat the Detroit Tigers in the World Series. Three years later, Dean suffered arm problems that cost him his blazing fastball and all but ended his career. He went on to become a famous broadcaster.

DID YOU KNOW?

Super Stat:

30

Wins for Dean in 1934. No NL pitcher has hit that milestone since.

Dizzy Dean had a memorable name, but his wasn't even the strangest of the Gashouse Gang members. That colorful Cardinals team featured Dean's brother Paul, who went by Daffy, plus a Dazzy (Vance), and a Ducky (Joe Medwick). Other players included Spud Davis, Ripper Collins (who knocked a league-high 35 homers), Kiddo Davis, and Tex Carleton. St. Louis won the World Series by taking the seventh game against Detroit 11–0.

FAST FACT: Ramirez has hit more playoff home runs than any other player, with 28.

Which slugger once disappeared into Fenway Park's Green Monster during a game?

When outfielder **Manny Ramirez** did something strange (which was pretty often), people would explain it by saying, "That's just Manny being Manny." He once refused to talk to the media during spring training. When he finally broke his silence, it was to tell them about a grill he was trying to sell. But the most Mannylike thing Ramirez did was to step into the Green Monster (the giant leftfield fence at Boston's Fenway Park). Sometimes he would drink Gatorade or talk on the phone. He usually did it during breaks in the game, but on July 18, 2005, he ventured into the Monster while Boston's pitching coach was visiting the mound—and he didn't return until the next pitch was being thrown. Ramirez had a simple explanation: He said he had to go to the bathroom.

FAST FACT: In his fourth career game, Syndergaard tied a team record for pitchers by getting three hits.

Which fireballing pitcher calls himself Thor?

He doesn't have a hammer with him when he pitches, but Noah Syndergaard takes his nickname seriously. He has posted several pictures of himself dressed as the superhero Thor. He got the name from a fan. "The home planet of Thor is called Asgard, which is like my last name," Syndergaard explained. "It just kind of stuck with me."

Syndergaard has embraced it. During the 2016 season, he hit the streets of New York City in his Thor outfit. He went up to a hot dog vendor and asked for "sustenance" before ordering "four of your finest boar." He also got into a taxi cab and told the driver to take him to Avengers Tower.

Like Thor, Syndergaard is strong. He's a serious weightlifter and can throw a ball almost 100 miles per hour. In 2016, he was tied for fourth in the National League with 218 strikeouts and third with an ERA of 2.60. Thor's strength is also evident at the plate. Syndergaard tied for the league lead for home runs by a pitcher by hitting three.

Super Stat:

0.5

Home runs per nine innings allowed by Syndergaard in 2016, making him the toughest pitcher in the NL to take deep.

Which Hall of Famer was known for his love of chicken?

Baseball players love their routines, but  Wade Boggs took the idea of doing the same thing every day to the extreme. The third baseman woke up at the same time every day, took batting practice at the same time, and took the same number of ground balls during practice. But his biggest superstition involved his pregame meal. Boggs ate chicken every day. He ate so much of the bird that his Boston Red Sox teammate Jim Rice called him Chicken Man. You can't really argue with the results. Boggs won five batting titles, hitting better than .350 each time. He retired as a member of the 3,000-hit club. And he amassed enough chicken recipes to write a book. Its name? *Fowl Tips*.

FAST FACT:
Boggs was also know for his love of cowboy boots. He missed several games in 1986 when he fell and hurt his ribs while trying to take off his boots.

Who celebrates Orioles wins by giving teammates a pie to the face?

If you come up with a big hit around Baltimore Orioles outfielder **Adam Jones,** be careful. In 2010, Jones began celebrating big plays by hitting the hero in the face with a shaving-cream pie. When Baltimore players complained that the shaving cream burned, a local bakery began delivering real (and tasty!) pies. Jones is the leader of the Orioles' pie brigade, but what happens if he comes up with a big play? (And he comes up with big plays a lot. Jones is a five-time All-Star and has hit at least 25 homers in a season six times.) "If I'm going to do it, I gotta be able to take it," he said. "If anybody pies me, I can't do anything about it but enjoy the pie."

Who became an international sensation when he came to the majors from Japan?

The biggest thing to hit baseball in 2001 was **Ichiro Suzuki.** The rightfielder had been one of the best hitters in Japan for years. When his team offered major league squads the chance to sign him, the Seattle Mariners jumped at the opportunity. Fans in the U.S. were intrigued by Ichiro, and fans back home in Japan couldn't wait to see how he fared against major league pitching. Ichiro was followed by a massive crowd of journalists—more than 100 of whom were Japanese—everywhere he played. Numerous fans flew to the United States from Japan to witness the sensation first hand.

Ichiro lived up to the hype. In his first season he was named the American League MVP after hitting .350 with 56 stolen bases. He became one of the game's most consistent hitters, amassing more than 3,000 major league hits. Combined with his 1,278 hits in Japan, Ichiro finished the 2016 season with more hits than any player in professional baseball history.

FAST FACT:
Ichiro is one of the few players in history to wear his first name on the back of his jersey.

DID YOU KNOW?

SONY

Ichiro wasn't the first player to cause fans in Japan to stop on the streets and watch his games on TV. But before he made his major league debut, all of the other players from Japan had been pitchers. The first, Masanori Murakami, played a little more than one season in the 1960s. The next was Hideo Nomo, who began his big league career in 1995. All told, there have been 56 players from Japan in Major League Baseball.

Super Stat:

262

Hits by Ichiro in 2004, a major league record. Of those, 225 were singles.

Which long-haired pitcher is known as the Freak?

When he was a freshman in high school, Tim Lincecum was just 4' 11" tall and weighed 85 pounds. He certainly wasn't going to overpower hitters, so he and his father decided they would come up with a pitching motion that would allow him to generate velocity. The little guy would take an incredibly long stride and wait until just before delivering the ball to unwind his body. It looked odd, but it worked. By the time he finished high school in 2003 Lincecum could throw 94 miles per hour—despite weighing 135 pounds.

His freakish delivery—coupled with his laid-back personality—earned Lincecum the nickname the Freak. And he was freakishly good. After joining the San Francisco Giants, he won the Cy Young Award in his first two full seasons and led the NL in strikeouts three times as he helped the team win three World Series.

Super Stat:

148

Pitches Lincecum threw in a no-hitter in 2013. It's the second-highest pitch count ever in a no-no.

Who was so fast that he could supposedly turn off the light and be in bed before the room got dark?

He might have been the fastest man ever to play baseball. But not many people saw him play. **Cool Papa Bell** spent 25 years in the Negro leagues and in foreign countries before African-American players were allowed in the majors. As a result, fans missed quite a show. Legendary pitcher Satchel Paige claimed that Bell once hit a line drive past his ear. "I turned around and saw the ball hit him sliding into second," Paige claimed. And then there was the story about the bedroom light, which was told by his former teammate Josh Gibson.

Bell was originally a pitcher, and his calmness on the mound earned him his nickname. He moved to centerfield, where he used his blazing speed to track down anything hit his way. In his career, Bell hit .337 in the Negro leagues, and he won the Triple Crown in the Mexican League in 1940. That year, eight of his 12 homers were inside-the-park.

What colorful speedster was known as the Man of Steal?

In 1982, **Rickey Henderson** of the Oakland A's stole 130 bases. That's two more steals than the A's had as a team in 2015 and 2016 combined. Henderson was the greatest base stealer of his day, and he'd gladly tell you that himself. The brash outfielder loved talking about himself—even though he usually spoke as if he were talking about someone else. For instance, he'd say, "Rickey wants to play baseball."

What Rickey mostly wanted to do was run. He had three seasons of 100 steals, and he swiped 25 for the San Diego Padres in 2001—when he was 42. When he retired, Henderson had 1,406 steals, or nearly 500 more than his closest competitor. He could also hit: Henderson was the AL MVP in 1990, when he batted .325 with 28 home runs.

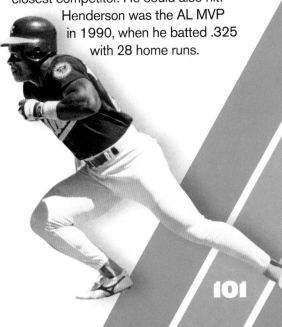

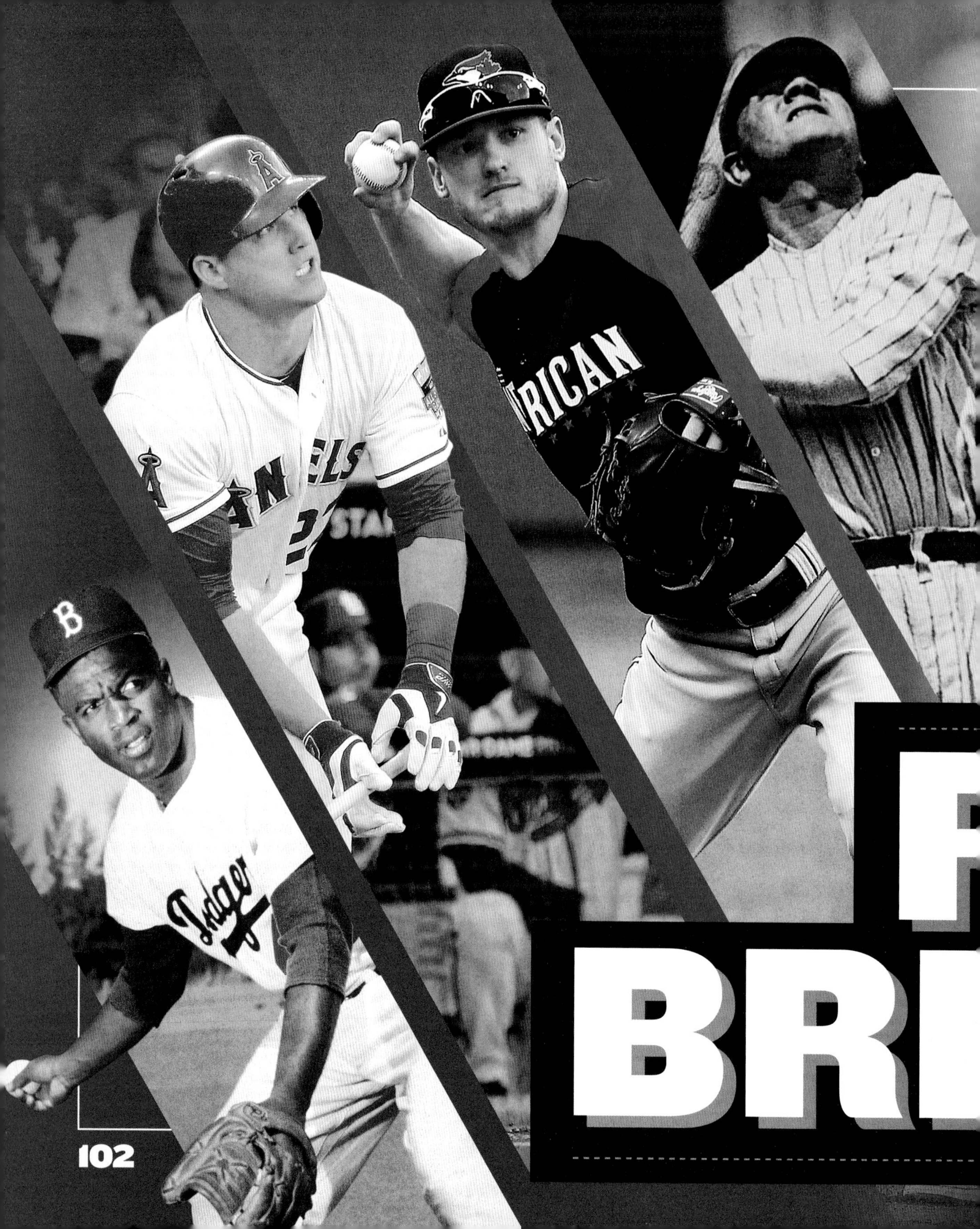

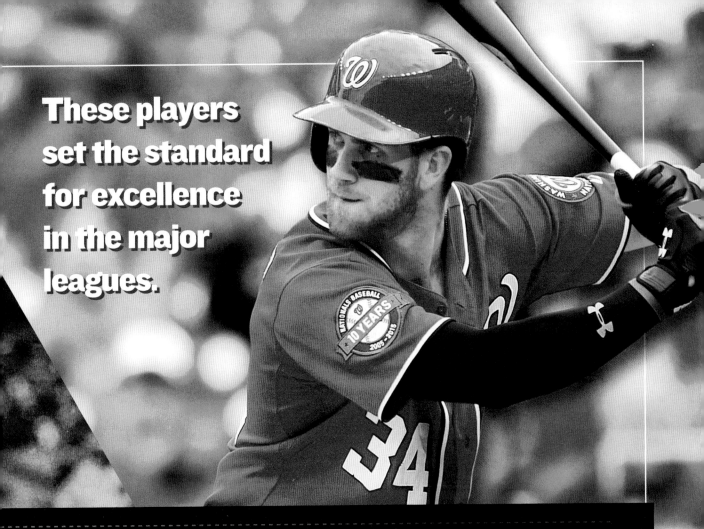

These players set the standard for excellence in the major leagues.

RECORD BREAKERS

Who was the first man to hit 30 (and 40, 50, and 60) homers?

Before Babe Ruth came along, teams scored runs by stringing together hits, bunting, and stealing bases. But the man known as the Sultan of Swat changed the way the game was played. He showed that swinging for the fences could lead to positive results. Ruth's home runs helped make the New York Yankees one of the game's great dynasties.

When Ruth joined the Yankees in 1920, he already owned the major league record for home runs in a season, with 29 in 1919 for the Boston Red Sox. In his first season with his new club, he broke that mark with his 30th in the team's 88th game. Ruth finished the season with 54. In 1927, he'd become the first man to hit 60 homers.

When his career was over, Ruth had won four World Series with the Yankees. And he had hit 714 home runs—or 336 more than anyone at that point.

Super Stat:

12

Season home-run titles won by Ruth, the most ever.

FAST FACT:
As a pitcher in 1916, Ruth won 23 games and led the American League in ERA.

Before he was a slugger for the Yankees, Ruth was a pitcher for the Boston Red Sox. He helped the Red Sox win three World Series in the 1910s. He eventually moved to the outfield so that Boston could take advantage of his bat.

Following the 1919 season, Red Sox owner Harry Frazee sold Ruth to New York. According to local lore, this led to a curse being placed on the Red Sox. Before Ruth went to the Yankees, they hadn't won a single championship. But after acquiring him, they won 26 titles. The Red Sox, meanwhile, struggled to win another. They finally broke "The Curse of the Bambino" in 2004, when they beat the St. Louis Cardinals to win their first World Series in 86 years.

FAST FACT: Harper made his first appearance on the cover of SPORTS ILLUSTRATED when he was 16.

Who was the youngest unanimous MVP?

When he was just 17, Bryce Harper was taken first overall in the 2010 draft by the Washington Nationals. A mere five years later, he put up a monster season that left no debate about who was the most valuable player in the NL.

Harper slugged 42 home runs and batted .330 in 2015. His on-base percentage was a staggering .460, and he led the league with 118 runs scored. When baseball writers voted for the MVP, every single one of them had Harper in first place. He became the 16th unanimous MVP pick—and, at age 22, the youngest.

Super Stat:

19

Harper's age when he made the 2012 All-Star Game, making him the youngest position player in the game's history.

Who pitched the most consecutive scoreless innings?

Late in the 1988 season, Los Angeles Dodgers pitcher **Orel Hershiser** got hot. Really hot. Beginning in the sixth inning of a game on August 30, he didn't allow a run until the first inning of the next season. His scoreless streak spanned 59 innings, beating the mark set by another Dodgers ace, Don Drysdale, by one inning. During the streak, opponents were hitless in 31 at bats with runners in scoring position. Hershiser finished the season with 23 wins and a 2.26 ERA.

FAST FACT: Hershiser became more aggressive after Dodgers manager Tommy Lasorda started calling him Bulldog.

Who was the last player to hit .400?

It's one of the most magical numbers in the game: .400. If a player posts that batting average, he's in truly elite company. In 1941, **Ted Williams** of the Boston Red Sox entered the last day of the season hitting .39955. Rounded up, that came to .400. But Williams wasn't satisfied. Instead of sitting out and making it to the milestone, he insisted on playing both games of a doubleheader. He got six hits in eight at bats, bringing his average to .406. Williams, who was nicknamed the Splendid Splinter, became just the ninth hitter to bat .400. And since he accomplished the feat, no one has come closer than .394.

FAST FACT:
In 2014, Stanton signed the richest contract in sports history, worth $325 million over 13 years.

Who hit the most homers in one Home Run Derby?

Against major league pitchers who are trying to get him out, Miami Marlins slugger **Giancarlo Stanton** hits home runs with great frequency. (In 2015, for instance, he hit 27 home runs—in just 74 games.) So imagine what he can do when he's facing someone who is grooving pitches right down the middle, like in the Home Run Derby, which is held during the All-Star break.

Stanton answered that question in 2016. During the course of the competition, he stroked an incredible 61 home runs. (The event was timed. Stanton hit his homers in 13½ minutes.) And he wasn't hitting pop flies that just made it over the fence. Stanton's home runs averaged a whopping 446 feet. The 61 homers traveled a total of 5.15 miles. And all 10 of the longest home runs hit during the competition came off of his bat. Said Oakland A's catcher Stephen Vogt, "That's superhuman."

Who threw the fastest pitch ever recorded?

The American League manager at the 2015 All-Star Game was Ned Yost of the Royals. During the game, he told one of his players, Kansas City third baseman Mike Moustakas, to grab a bat and pinch hit against **Aroldis Chapman** of the Cincinnati Reds. After the game Moustakas jokingly said of Yost, "I thought we had a good relationship!"

You can't blame Moustakas for not wanting to face Chapman. The lefty is the hardest thrower the game has ever seen. That's been obvious since his rookie season. In his 11th appearance, he threw 25 pitches against the San Diego Padres. Every single one of them was faster than 100 miles per hour. But one heater he threw to Tony Gwynn, Jr. had a little extra on it. It was measured at 105.1 miles per hour, the fastest pitch in history. "I didn't see it until the ball was behind me," Gwynn said.

FAST FACT:
Chapman defected from Cuba while playing in a competition in the Netherlands.

Super Stat:
52.5
Percentage of batters Chapman struck out in 2014, the highest in history.

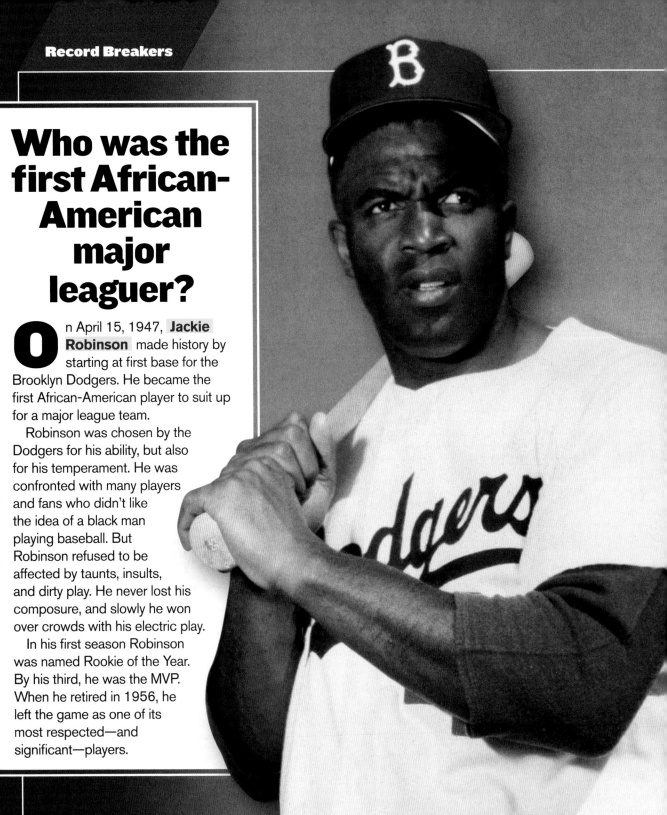

Who was the first African-American major leaguer?

On April 15, 1947, Jackie Robinson made history by starting at first base for the Brooklyn Dodgers. He became the first African-American player to suit up for a major league team.

Robinson was chosen by the Dodgers for his ability, but also for his temperament. He was confronted with many players and fans who didn't like the idea of a black man playing baseball. But Robinson refused to be affected by taunts, insults, and dirty play. He never lost his composure, and slowly he won over crowds with his electric play.

In his first season Robinson was named Rookie of the Year. By his third, he was the MVP. When he retired in 1956, he left the game as one of its most respected—and significant—players.

Super Stat:

4

Sports that Robinson received letters in at UCLA: baseball, football, basketball, and track.

FAST FACT: Robinson's number 42 has been retired by all of professional baseball, so no player will wear it again.

DID YOU KNOW?

Some of Robinson's own teammates didn't want to play alongside him because of his race. But their attitudes changed when they realized how good Robinson was. Before he made his debut in 1947, the Dodgers had been to the World Series only three times and had lost all of them. But they won the pennant six times in Robinson's 10 seasons. And in 1955, Brooklyn won its only World Series. Robinson wasn't the only African American to make an impact with the Dodgers. The World Series–winning team featured Robinson at third base, catcher Roy Campanella (the National League MVP who hit .318 with 32 home runs), and pitcher Don Newcombe (20 wins and a 3.20 ERA).

Who was the youngest slugger to hit 50 home runs in a season?

When he was in the minor leagues in 2004, **Prince Fielder** said, "I don't consider myself a power hitter." Well, if he's not a power hitter, then no one is. That season, the big guy hit 23 home runs in Double A at the age of 20. Two years later he was in the major leagues, hitting 28 bombs for the Milwaukee Brewers. But in his second full season, Fielder hit a historic number of home runs. On September 25, 2007, he hit two homers against the St. Louis Cardinals to give him 50 for the year. That made him just the 25th player to reach that milestone, joining his father, Cecil, who did it in 1990 for the Detroit Tigers. Prince was just 23 at the time, making him the youngest member of the 50-homer club.

FAST FACT: Fielder, who was forced to retire due to injuries in 2016, finished his career with 319 home runs—the same number as his father.

Who had baseball's longest hitting streak?

For two months during the 1941 season, **Joe DiMaggio** of the New York Yankees never had an off day. He got a hit in 56 consecutive games, easily the longest in major league history. (It wasn't Joltin' Joe's longest, though. In the minors he once hit in 61 straight games.) DiMaggio's streak finally came to an end on July 17 against the Cleveland Indians. Tribe third baseman Ken Keltner made two terrific plays in the field to rob DiMaggio of a pair of hits. The next day, DiMaggio got two hits, beginning another streak that lasted 16 games. That means during the summer of 1941, DiMaggio hit safely in 72 out of 73 games. Since the end of his streak, no one has had a run longer than 44 games.

Super Stat:

7

Seasons in which DiMaggio had more home runs than strikeouts, a major league record.

FAST FACT:
DiMaggio had two brothers, Vince and Dom, who were also major leaguers.

Who got the most All-Star votes in a single year?

Canada has some serious baseball fans, but sports buffs in the country love hockey. That was shown once again in 2015, when **Josh Donaldson** of the Toronto Blue Jays was in the midst of a great season but was trailing in the All-Star vote. Hockey announcer Don Cherry, who is one of the most recognizable faces in Canada, began campaigning for Donaldson. Fans all over the country took notice. Donaldson had been trailing Mike Moustakas of the Kansas City Royals in the contest to be the starting third baseman for the American League. With the boost from Cherry, Donaldson overtook Moustakas and amassed a record 14,090,188 votes. Donaldson went on to be named the league's Most Valuable Player in 2015.

FAST FACT: Donaldson is an avid collector of baseball cards and memorabilia. His mom once drove him six hours so he could get a player's autograph.

DID YOU KNOW?

The All-Star Game was designed to be an exhibition highlighting the top players in each league. The results only mattered for bragging rights. But in 2002, the game ended in a tie because both teams ran out of players in the 11th inning. Fans were outraged. The league and players decided that if there was something riding on the outcome of the game, the managers would take winning more seriously. So for the next 15 years, the league that won the All-Star Game got home-field advantage in that year's World Series. Starting in 2017, the league champion with the better record gets home-field advantage in the Fall Classic.

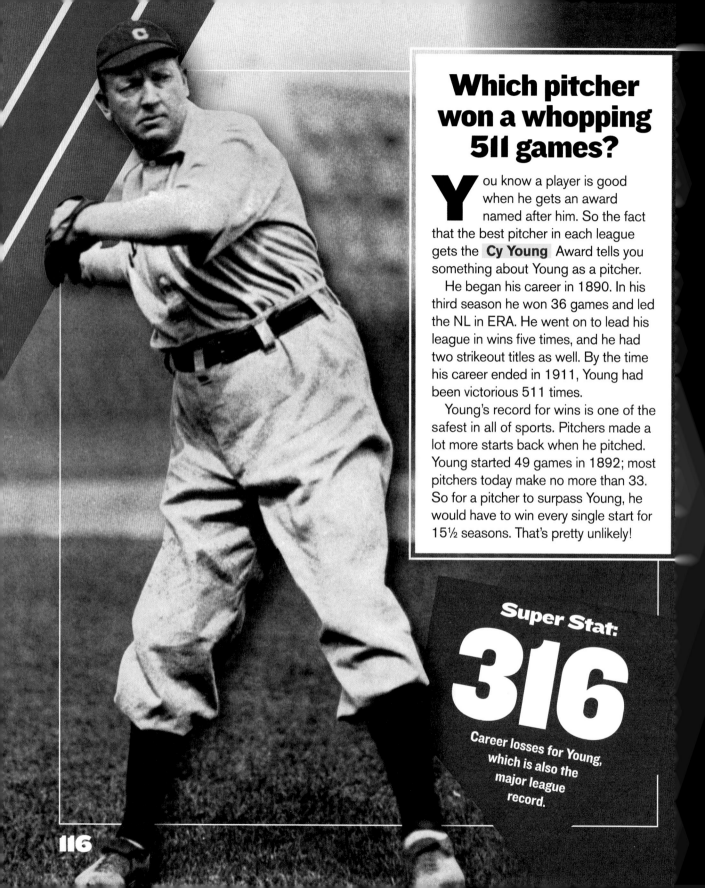

Which pitcher won a whopping 511 games?

You know a player is good when he gets an award named after him. So the fact that the best pitcher in each league gets the Cy Young Award tells you something about Young as a pitcher.

He began his career in 1890. In his third season he won 36 games and led the NL in ERA. He went on to lead his league in wins five times, and he had two strikeout titles as well. By the time his career ended in 1911, Young had been victorious 511 times.

Young's record for wins is one of the safest in all of sports. Pitchers made a lot more starts back when he pitched. Young started 49 games in 1892; most pitchers today make no more than 33. So for a pitcher to surpass Young, he would have to win every single start for 15½ seasons. That's pretty unlikely!

Super Stat:

316

Career losses for Young, which is also the major league record.

Which batter has the most hits in major league history?

They called him Charlie Hustle for a good reason. **Pete Rose** always played as hard as he could, and it paid off in a big way. On September 11, 1985, Rose got career hit number 4,192, breaking Ty Cobb's 60-year-old career record. Rose was 44 years old.

In his 24-year career—spent mostly with the Cincinnati Reds—Rose had at least 200 hits 10 times. He was a three-time batting champ, and he was named the National League's Most Valuable Player in 1973.

After breaking Cobb's record, Rose played one more season. On August 14, 1986, he collected three hits against the San Francisco Giants. That left him with 4,256 for his career—a number that hitters will be chasing for years to come.

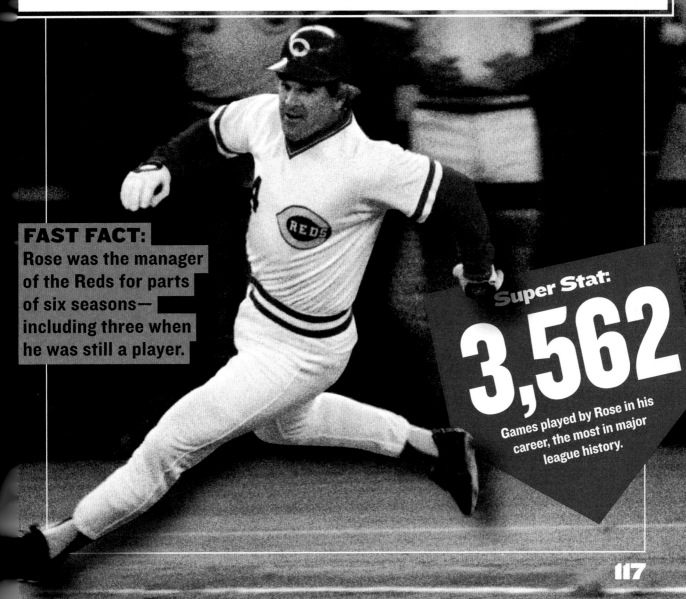

FAST FACT:
Rose was the manager of the Reds for parts of six seasons— including three when he was still a player.

Super Stat:
3,562
Games played by Rose in his career, the most in major league history.

117

Which iron man appeared in the most consecutive games?

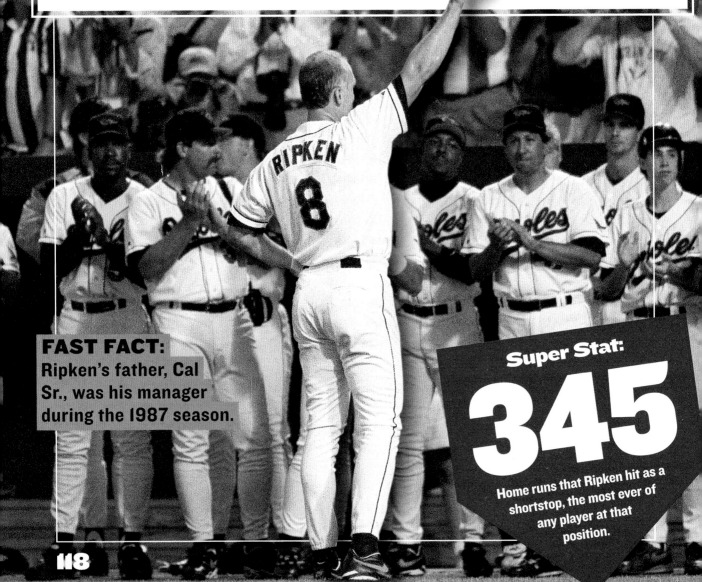

The 1980s and 1990s were not a good time to be a shortstop in the Baltimore Orioles organization. Chances of getting onto the field were pretty hard to come by thanks to **Cal Ripken, Jr.** Beginning on May 30, 1982, Ripken didn't miss a game for more than 16 years. (Later in the streak he moved from shortstop to third base.) When he finally took himself out of the lineup, he had played in 2,632 games in a row—or 502 more than the previous record holder, Lou Gehrig. Ripken didn't just play. He played at an exceptional level. He was the AL MVP in 1982 and 1991. Ripken finished his career with 3,184 hits and an astonishing 19 straight All-Star Game appearances.

FAST FACT: Ripken's father, Cal Sr., was his manager during the 1987 season.

Super Stat:

345

Home runs that Ripken hit as a shortstop, the most ever of any player at that position.

Who was the oldest rookie in history?

Most rookies are relatively young players. That wasn't the case for **Satchel Paige.** The righthanded pitcher was 42 years old when he made his major league debut with the Cleveland Indians in 1948.

Paige had spent more than 20 years playing in the Negro leagues when black players were not allowed in the major leagues. Paige was a hard-throwing righthander who was known for being energetic, and he was one of the most quotable players in baseball. (His most famous saying was probably "Don't look back. Something might be gaining on you.")

When he joined the Indians, Paige was well past his prime. But he was still effective. He was 6–1 in his rookie season with an ERA of 2.48. He helped the Indians win the American League. He later signed with the St. Louis Browns and made two AL All-Star teams—when he was 45 and 46 years old.

Who has the record for the most saves in a season?

Alex Rodriguez is known as A-Rod, and **Francisco Rodriguez** is K-Rod. The letter K is the symbol for strikeout, and Rodriguez picked up the nickname during the 2002 playoffs. As an unknown setup man who had spent almost the entire season in the minors, Rodriguez notched 28 strikeouts in 18⅔ innings.

Three years later Rodriguez became the Angels' full-time closer. He was an immediate success, leading the league in saves his first two seasons. But K-Rod's best campaign was 2008, when he set a major league record with 62 saves.

Who is the only player to be named MVP in back-to-back All-Star Games?

The All-Star Game features the best of the best. So what does that say about a guy who is named Most Valuable Player of the Game twice in a row? Probably that he's pretty special.

That certainly describes Mike Trout. In the 2014 Midsummer Classic, the Los Angeles Angels centerfielder banged a double and a triple, and drove in two runs. He was named MVP. The following year he hit a leadoff home run in the top of the first to win the award again. He became just the fourth player to win the award twice, and the first to do it consecutively.

Trout isn't just an amazing hitter. He's also a great base runner. In fact, he reached 100 stolen bases before he hit his 100th home run. When he finally hit homer number 100, he became the youngest member of the 100-100 club. He was 23 years, 253 days—nearly two months younger than Alex Rodriguez.

Trout's combination of speed and hitting ability has wowed fans—and his fellow players. Said former Angels teammate Vernon Wells, "If people wanted to build a perfect baseball player in a video game, this is what you'd want your guy to look like."

Super Stat:

2

Lowest position that Trout has finished in the AL MVP race since his first full season in 2012.

FAST FACT:
Trout was so dangerous in high school that he was once intentionally walked with the bases loaded.

Who has the highest career batting average?

Something funny happened in 1917. Someone other than Ty Cobb won the American League batting title. Cobb had the league's best average 12 times in a 13-year span. The only time he didn't win it, in 1917, he finished second, with a .371 average.

Cobb retired in 1928 after a 24-season career. In 23 of those seasons, he had a batting average of .316 or better. His career mark was .366. That's the highest ever. In fact, in the past 20 years, only seven players have managed to hit as high as .366 in a single season. And once he reached base on a hit, Cobb was dangerous. His mark of 892 stolen bases stood for 49 years.

Super Stat:

54

Times that Cobb stole home in his career. The all-time stolen base leader, Rickey Henderson, only did it four times.

Which catcher threw out the highest percentage of base stealers?

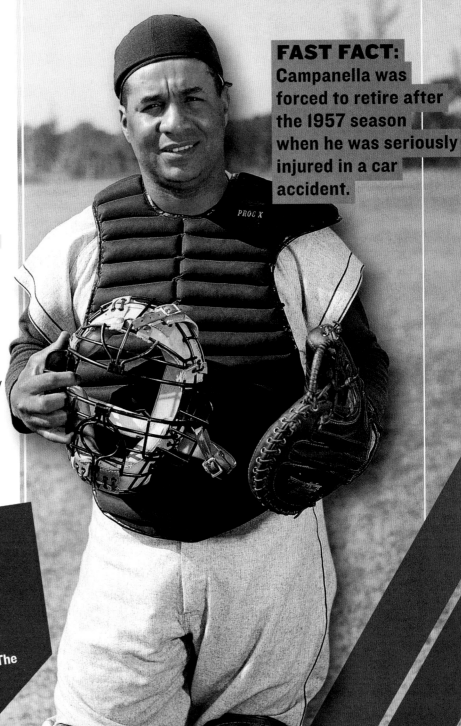

Few catchers have ever been as good at getting on base as **Roy Campanella.** And no one has been as good at erasing other team's runners.

The slugger spent eight years in the Negro leagues before joining the Brooklyn Dodgers. It didn't take long for opponents to realize that running on Campy was a bad idea. The ones who were foolish enough to try weren't likely to succeed. The three-time MVP threw out 57% of would-be base stealers in his career, a major league record.

FAST FACT: Campanella was forced to retire after the 1957 season when he was seriously injured in a car accident.

Super Stat:

142

RBIs for Campanella in 1953. The only catcher with more in one season is Johnny Bench in 1970.

Who had the highest career average when hitting with two strikes?

When a pitcher gets two strikes on a hitter, he usually feels pretty good. Unless that hitter was **Tony Gwynn.**

Most hitters get defensive when they're behind in the count, but Gwynn was dangerous no matter the count. In his career he had a batting average of .302 with two strikes. That's easily the highest since the stat began being kept in 1988. (For the 2016 season the league batting average in two-strike situations was .176.)

Gwynn's hitting prowess was legendary. He had excellent vision and could quickly identify what kind of pitch was coming. He could hit the ball to any part of the field, and he spent countless hours studying videotape. The end result: Gwynn won eight batting titles with the San Diego Padres.

FAST FACT:
Gwynn played four seasons of college basketball at San Diego State. He later became the school's baseball coach.

Super Stat:

.394

Gwynn's batting average in 1994, the closest anyone has come to hitting .400 since Ted Wiliams did it in 1941.

Who has won the most Platinum Gloves?

Every season, the top fielding player at each position in the American and National Leagues is awarded a Gold Glove. But there is a metal that's more precious than gold: platinum. So the top fielder overall in each league is given the Platinum Glove. Since the award was first handed out in 2011, catcher **Yadier Molina** of the St. Louis Cardinals has dominated. He has won the award four times; no one else has won more than two.

Molina, who has two brothers who also caught in the majors, is known for his strong arm, which has cut down many opposing base stealers. He also is a master at calling pitches and framing close ones to make them look like strikes.

Super Stat:

5

Seasons in which Molina has had a batting average of at least .300.

Player Index

Cover: Illustration by Artistic Image/AA Reps Inc.
Front Cover: Jason Miller/Getty Images (Trout); Damian Strohmeyer (Rivera); NY Daily News Archive/Getty Images (Mays); Martin Paul/Getty Images (baseball); Score RF/Getty Images (background)
Page 2-3: Damian Strohmeyer (Jeter); St. Louis Cardinals Archive/Getty Images (Smith); Walter Iooss, Jr. (Ripken Jr., Aaron); Chris Carlson/AP (Kershaw)
Page 4-5: Harry How/Getty Images (Johnson); Walter Iooss, Jr. (Gibson); James Drake (Mantle); Robert Beck (Ortiz); V.J. Lovero (Jeter)
Page 6-7: John Biever
Page 8: Mark Kauffman
Page 9: Robert Beck
Page 10: Neil Leifer (Seaver); AP (Larsen)
Page 11: Jamie Squire/Getty Images
Page 12-13: Matt York/AFP/Getty Images
Page 14: Focus on Sport/Getty Images
Page 15: Damian Strohmeyer
Page 16-17: Damian Strohmeyer
Page 18: Rob Carr/Getty Images
Page 19: John Biever
Page 20: Jim Mone/AP
Page 21: Rogers Photo Archive/Getty Images (Podres); Neil Leifer (Ford)
Page 22: Neil Leifer
Page 23: Focus on Sport/Getty Images
Page 24-25: Focus on Sport/Getty Images
Page 26: Al Tielemans
Page 27: John Iacono
Page 28-29: Walter Iooss, Jr. (Aaron); Jonathan Daniel/Getty Images (Bryant); Phil Long/AP (Cabrero); National Baseball Hall of Fame Library, Cooperstown, NY (Gehrig); Albert Dickson/Sporting News/Getty Images (Griffey Jr.)
Page 30: Al Tielemans
Page 31: Greg Nelson
Page 32-33: Focus On Sport/Getty Images (Aaron); Tony Triolo (Aaron inset)
Page 34: Jerry Wachter
Page 35: AP
Page 36: AP
Page 37: David Banks/Getty Images
Page 38-39: Bill Chan/AP
Page 40-41: Mark Rucker/Transcendental Graphics/Getty Images
Page 42-43: Robert Beck (Bonds); Al Tielemans (Bonds inset)
Page 44: Peter Read Miller
Page 45: Louis Requena/MLB Photos/Getty Images
Page 46: Kidwiler Collection/Diamond Images/Getty Images (Kiner); David Durochik/AP (Winfield)

Page 47: Photo File/Getty Images
Page 48: Mark Rucker/Transcendental Graphics/Getty Images
Page 49: Al Tielemans
Page 50: Jennifer Stewart/Getty Images (Arenado); Mark Rucker/Transcendental Graphics/Getty Images (Baker)
Page 51: Jim McIsaac/Getty Images
Page 52-53: Neil Leifer (Mays); NY Daily News Archive/Getty Images (Mays inset)
Page 54-55: Robert Beck (Kershaw); Underwood Archives/Getty Images (Johnson); Al Tielemans (Martinez); Rich Pilling/MLB Photos/Getty Images (Ryan); Mitchell Leff/Getty Images (Scherzer)
Page 56-57: Neil Leifer (Koufax); Mark Cunningham/MLB Photos/Getty Images (Cy Young award)
Page 58: AP
Page 59: V.J. Lovero
Page 60-61: Bob Rosato
Page 62: John Iacono
Page 63: Bob Rosato
Page 64: Bob Rosato
Page 65: Jim McIsaac/Getty Images
Page 66-67: Lou Capozzola (Martinez); Sporting News/Getty Images (Martinez inset)
Page 68-69: Manny Millan
Page 70: Rob Foldy/Getty Images
Page 71: Mark Kauffman
Page 72: David E. Klutho
Page 73: Mark Rucker/Transcendental Graphics/Getty Images (Radbourn); Heinz Kluetmeier (Carlton)
Page 74: Sporting News/Getty Images
Page 75: G Fiume/Getty Images
Page 76: John W. McDonough (Halladay); Rich Pilling/MLB Photos/Getty Images (Gossage)
Page 77: Tom Mihalek/AFP/Getty Images
Page 78-79: Photo File/MLB Photos/Getty Images (Berra); Neil Leifer (Fingers); AP (Smith); Patrick McDermott/Getty Images (Jones); Christian Petersen/Getty Images (Wilson)
Page 80: AP
Page 81: Eric Risberg/AP
Page 82-83: AP
Page 84: Heinz Kluetmeier
Page 85: Mark Rucker/Transcendental Graphics/Getty Images (Wagner); Kathy Willens/AP (Wagner card)
Page 86: Herb Scharfman/Sports Imagery/Getty Images (Fidrych); AP (Fingers)
Page 87: Focus on Sport/Getty Images
Page 88-89: Rick Stewart/Getty Images (Sanders baseball); Joseph Patronite/Getty Images (Sanders football)

Page 90: Robert Beck
Page 91: St. Louis Cardinals Archive/Getty Images
Page 92: AP (Dean); Mark Rucker/Transcendental Graphics/Getty Images (Gashouse Gang)
Page 93: Damian Strohmeyer
Page 94-95: Jim McIsaac/Getty Images
Page 96: Ron Vesely/MLB Photos/Getty Images
Page 97: Rob Carr/Getty Images
Page 98-99: John Mabanglo/AFP/Getty Images (Suzuki); Koji Sasahara/AP (Japan fans)
Page 100: Robert Beck
Page 101: Sporting News/Getty Images (Bell); Focus on Sport/Getty Images (Henderson)
Page 102-103: Photo File/MLB Photos/Getty Images (Robinson); Rob Carr/Getty Images (Trout, Donaldson); Iconic Archive/Getty Images (Ruth); Mitchell Layton/Getty Images (Harper)
Page 104-105: Transcendental Graphics/Getty Images (Ruth); The Stanley Weston Archive/Getty Images (Ruth with Red Sox)
Page 106: G Fiume/Getty Images
Page 107: Stephen Dunn/Getty Images
Page 108: Mark Kauffman (Williams); Harry How/Getty Images (Stanton)
Page 109: David Kohl/AP
Page 110-111: Photo File/MLB Photos/Getty Images (Robinson); The Stanley Weston Archive/Getty Images (Robinson with teammates)
Page 112: Morry Gash/AP
Page 113: The Stanley Weston Archive/Getty Images
Page 114-115: Brace Hemmelgarn/Minnesota Twins/Getty Images (Donaldson); Andy Lyons/Getty Images (All-Star game)
Page 116: National Baseball Hall of Fame Library/MLB Photos/Getty Images
Page 117: AP
Page 118: John Iacono
Page 119: George Silk/Time Life Pictures/Getty Images (Paige); Frank Specker/AP (Rodriguez)
Page 120-121: Mark Cunningham/MLB Photos/Getty Images (Trout); Rob Carr/Getty Images (Trout inset)
Page 122: Iconic Archive/Getty Images
Page 123: AP
Page 124: MLB Photos/Getty Images
Page 125: Rob Leiter/MLB Photos/Getty Images
Back Cover: Stephen Green (Bryant); AP (Smith); Hy Peskin (Williams); Jim McIsaac/Getty Images (Kershaw)